GLOBE EDUCATION SHAKESPEARE

FOR **EDUQAS** GCSE ENGLISH LITERATURE

ROMEO AND JULIET

William Shakespeare

HODDER
EDUCATION
AN HACHETTE UK COMPANY

Shakespeare and the Globe

Shakespeare was born in 1564, in Stratford, a small town in the Midlands. We know he was still in Stratford as an eighteen-year old, when he got married. By 1592, he had moved to London, become an actor, and become a playwright. Shakespeare died in Stratford in 1616. He probably retired three or four years earlier, having bought land, and the biggest house in the town

Shakespeare was successful. ▓▓▓▓▓▓▓▓▓▓▓ acti▓▓ company, and a sharehold▓▓▓▓▓▓▓▓▓▓▓▓ 1599. His company was the ▓▓▓▓▓▓▓▓▓▓▓▓ made them his company in 160▓ ▓ey ▓▓▓▓ ▓▓▓ ▓▓e King's Men. Men, because women were not allowed to act on the stage. Boys or men played all the women's parts. Shakespeare wrote at least 40 plays, of which 38 survive. Only eighteen of his plays were printed in his lifetime, including *Romeo and Juliet*. The others only survive because, after his death, his colleagues published a collection of 36 of his plays, known as the *First Folio*.

London Theatres

There were professional companies of actors working in London from the middle of the sixteenth century. They usually performed in inns, and the city council often tried to ban them. The solution was to have their own purpose-built theatre, just outside the area the council controlled. The first, simply called *The Theatre*, opened in 1576.

Shakespeare's Globe today

Sam Wanamaker, an American actor and director, founded the Shakespeare's Globe Trust in 1970. Sam could not understand why there wasn't a proper memorial to the world's greatest playwright in the city where he had lived and worked. He started fundraising to build a new Globe Theatre. Sadly, Sam died before the theatre opened in 1997.

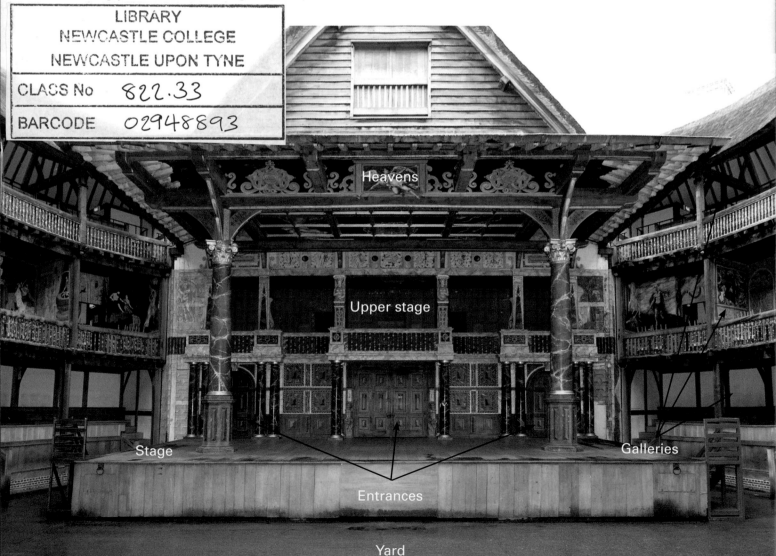

Heavens

Upper stage

Stage

Galleries

Entrances

Yard

The new Globe is the third. The first burnt down in 1613 during a performance of Shakespeare's Henry VIII. The King's Men rebuilt it on the same site, and it re-opened in 1614. This second one was closed in 1642, and pulled down in 1647 to build houses.

The new Globe is 200 yards from the original site, and is based on all the evidence that survives. It has been built using the same materials as the original, and using the same building techniques.

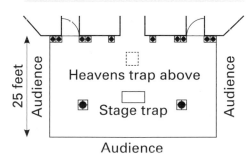

The stage trap opened into the area under the stage. The heavens trap was not on the stage, but above it. Actors playing gods might be lowered down to the stage through it.

The first Globe Theatre

The Globe Theatre was open air. If it rained, some of the audience got wet. There was no special lighting; so the plays were performed in the afternoon, in daylight. This meant that, unlike most modern theatres, the actors could see the audience, as well as the audience see the actors (and each other). It may have held as many as 3,000 people, with, perhaps, 1,000 standing in the yard. Those standing paid one old penny (there were 240 in £1). The rest sat in the three galleries, so they were under cover if it rained. They paid more, at least two pence, and as much as six pence for the best seats. The audience was a mixture of social classes, with the poorer people standing.

The stage was large, and extended into the middle of the yard, so there were people on three sides. We think it had three entrances in the back wall – a door on either side, and a larger one in the middle. There was a roof so the actors, and their expensive costumes, would always be in the dry. The underside of this roof, called *the heavens*, was painted with the signs of the zodiac. There was also an upper stage, which was sometimes used in plays, sometimes used by the musicians, and also had the most expensive seats in the theatre. All the rest of the audience could see people who sat in the upper stage area. If you sat there, people could see who you were, that you could afford to sit there, and your expensive clothes.

The **play text** is the place to start. What characters say is in black, and stage directions are in blue. Line numbers, on the right, help you refer to an exact place.

Unwieldy, slow, heavy, and pale as lead.

Enter Nurse and Peter.

O God, she comes! O honey nurse, what news?
Hast thou met with him? Send thy man away.

Nurse   Peter, stay at the gate.   *[Exit Peter.]* 20

Some **stage directions**, like the second one above, have square brackets. This means they are not in the original text, but have been added to help you when you read. They tell you what you would see on the stage.

17-8 **For nought ... special good
doth give:** there's nothing that
doesn't have some good to it

The **glossary** is right next to the text. To help you find the word or phrase you want, each entry has the line number in blue, then the word or phrase in black, and finally the explanation in blue again. To keep it clear, sometimes, as in this case, some words from the original have been missed out, and replaced with three dots.

Actor's view boxes are exactly what they say. Actors who have played the part at the Globe tell you what they thought about their character and some of their choices.

There are lots of **photos** of productions of the play at Shakespeare's Globe. You'll notice different productions look very different. This is because each creative team and cast interpret the text. And remember, Shakespeare wrote to be interpreted by actors, and to have his plays watched, not read. The captions (on green boxes) tell you what you are looking at, and give you a question to think about. Unless the question says otherwise, the answer will be in the play text on the opposite page. The names of the actors are in smaller print.

From the Rehearsal Room gives you versions of the exercises actors use during rehearsals to help them understand the play. They come with questions that help you reflect on what you can learn from the exercise. **Working Cuts** sometimes go with the From the Rehearsal Room activities. They cut lines from the scene so you can do the activity in the time you have available.

Shakespeare's World boxes give you important context for the play. For example, what most people at the time thought about marriage is different from what most people think today. If you understand the difference, it helps you to understand how the characters think about marriage in the play.

Director's Notes boxes come at the end of every scene. They give you a quick summary of the most important things in the scene, and a focus to think about.

Looking forward to the Exam

To help you get ready for the exam, parts of the book are written by experienced examiners. Turn the page (to pages 6–7) to find a explanation of how the exam works. This is a good place to start. Then, while you are working on the play, there are two special features to help.

exam SKILLS

Target skill: analysis of a character's language and role

Question: How does Shakespeare present the Friar in this speech?

Shakespeare often uses friars in his plays as people who suggest plans. Here the Friar tries to take on the role of *deus ex machina* (a power that comes in the nick of time to solve a difficulty). He is a plot vehicle whose role here furthers the action of the play and helps us to understand Romeo's character. Read the Shakespeare's World section on secret marriage, to help you appreciate the significance of consummating an illegal marriage, and to understand why the Friar helps Romeo to spend the night with Juliet.

1 With a partner:
  • Count the questions in lines 110–120.
  • Count how many times the Friar uses triple references (groups of three) as in "thy shape, thy love, thy wit".
  • Identify the similes ("Like powder…").
  • Find the repetition in lines 135–145.
  How does Shakespeare use these techniques to encourage Romeo to listen to the speech?

2 The tone of the Friar's speech changes at line 148 ("Go get thee to thy love…"). *What do you notice about the verbs in this section of the speech? Find all the Friar's imperatives (instructions) telling Romeo how to act. How do they influence the mood of the scene?*

3 How far do you agree with the statements below? Decide which you agree with most and least.
  a) The Friar's diatribe is so insulting that the audience will find it hard to think Romeo deserves to survive and thrive.
  b) The Friar succeeds in diverting Romeo's thoughts of suicide and makes him act positively.
  c) The Friar's speech is useful in plot terms because it informs the audience while advising Romeo.

4 How do the insights you have gained help you answer the question above?

Exam skills boxes focus on the skills you need to do well. They start by telling you the skill you are going to practice, then give you a question with some of the same demands as the question you will get in the exam. What follows is a mixture of explanation, example, and some things for you to think about and practice.

exam PREPARATION

Text focus: Act 4 Scene 3 lines 15–57

(AO1) Response to characters and events:
• When the need for comfort almost overwhelms her, Juliet starts to call for the Nurse, not for her mother. *Why do you think she calls for the Nurse's comfort after being let down by her in Act 3 Scene 5?*
• Juliet runs through the possible problems in her mind and verbalises them for the audience. Her fears remind us of both her youth and her maturity. *Find evidence of both.*
• Juliet has a dagger with her in case she needs it but doesn't work. *Do you think that she would commit suicide?*
• The eventual decision to drink the draught comes quite suddenly, provoked by the image of Tybalt's ghost seeking out Romeo for vengeance. *Why do you think she drinks the draught at this point?*
• Arrange these events in the order they take place in the soliloquy:
  1 Juliet fears being suffocated by the vault's stale air.
  2 Juliet fears seeing her ancestors' ghosts in the vault.
  3 She imagines Tybalt's ghost trying to kill Romeo.
  4 Juliet feels cold with fear.
  5 She wants company, before realising this is a task that she can only do alone.
  6 Juliet fears that the draught is a poison to kill her.

(AO2) Language, structure and form:
• The speech is a soliloquy, outlining Juliet's fears. *Why might Shakespeare have chosen to give her a soliloquy here rather than just continuing the play's action?*
• Read lines 15–16. *Which words evoke anxiety and cold? What do they reveal about Juliet's state of mind?*
• Juliet uses the interrogative mood (questions) then moves to an exclamatory mood towards the end. *Find examples and comment on the effect created.*
• Look at the sentence length of lines 35–49. *What effect does this create?*
• Shakespeare evokes the terror of the Capulet tomb by giving us, through Juliet's imagination, images of dead bodies. *Find examples and comment on what they convey about Juliet's state of mind.*

Question:
How does Shakespeare present Juliet in this part of the play? (15 marks)

Advice: Linking character points to wider thematic issues in the play can help to strengthen your answers. *Consider in what ways this extract tells us more about the themes of:*
• love, • death, • parents and children, • power.

Exam preparation boxes help you practice for the exam. Your exam question starts with an extract from the play, and here you can see you are given a text focus, with about 40 lines. Read these lines first and carefully (just like you will need to read the extract first and carefully in the exam).

In the Exam your answer will be marked against three objectives (see pages 6–7). Here you are shown some of the sorts of things you can do for each objective, and given some ideas to think about and practice on. Finally you get the question, which is like one of the different types of question as you will get in the exam. With the work and thinking you have done before, you will be in a good position to answer it.

The Characters in the play

This book uses photographs from three productions of *Romeo and Juliet* at Shakespeare's Globe. The actors and creative teams of each production are an important part of the book.

	2004 *Director:* *Tim Carroll*	**spring 2009** *Director:* *Bill Buckhurst*	**summer 2009** *Director: Dominic Dromgoole*	**2013** *Director:* *Bill Buckhurst*
Prince Escalus, ruler of Verona	Joel Trill	Nicholas Khan	Andrew Vincent	Emma Pallant
Mercutio, related to the Prince	James Garnon	Shane Zaza	Philip Cumbus	Richard James-Neale
Paris, also related to the Prince	Callum Coates	Nicholas Khan	Tom Stuart	Tom Whitelock
The Capulets				
Capulet, head of the house	Bill Stewart	Vincent Brimble	Ian Redford	Jason Baughan
Lady Capulet, his wife	Melanie Jessop	Golda Rosheuvel	Miranda Foster	Emma Pallant
Juliet, their daughter	Kananu Kirimi	Lorraine Burroughs	Ellie Kendrick	Jade Anouka
Tybalt, her cousin	Simon Müller	Marshall Griffin	Ukweli Roach	Beruce Khan
Nurse, to Juliet	Bette Bourne	Jane Bertish	Penny Layden	Lisa Stevenson
Peter, a servant of the Capulets	John Paul Connolly	Nicholas Khan	Fergal McElherron	Dickon Tyrrell
Cousin, to Capulet				
Petruchio, follower of Tybalt				
Sampson, a servant of the Capulets		Lorraine Burroughs	James Lailey	
Gregory, a servant of the Capulets	Callum Coates	James Alexandrou	Fergal McElherron	Richard James-Neale
The Montagues				
Montague, head of the house	Terry McGinty	Colin Hurley	Michael O'Hagan	Dickon Tyrrell
Lady Montague, his wife	Julia Marsen	Jane Bertish	Holly Atkins	
Romeo, their son	Tom Burke	James Alexandrou	Adetomiwa Edun	Will Featherstone
Benvolio, Romeo's friend	Rhys Meredith	Ben Aldridge	Jack Farthing	Josh Williams
Balthasar, Romeo's servant	Tas Emiabata		Fergal McElherron	
Abraham, servant of the Montagues		Shane Zaza	Graham Vick	
Friar Lawrence	John McEnery	Colin Hurley	Rawiri Paratene	Dickon Tyrrell
Friar John	Rhys Meredith	Marshall Griffin	James Lailey	Richard James-Neale
An Apothecary, in Manuta	Terry McGinty	Shane Zaza	Graham Vick	Beruce Khan
Servants				
Officers of the Watch		Ben Aldridge		
Citizens				
Designer	Jenny Tiramani	Ben Stones	Simon Daw	Hannah Clark
Composer	Claire van Kampen	Olly Fox	Nigel Hess	Alex Silverman
Choreographer	Siân Williams	Siân Williams	Siân Williams	Georgina Lamb
Fight Director	Rodney Cottier & Jonathan Waller	Alison de Burgh	Malcolm Ranson	Kevin McCurdy
Musical Director	William Lyons & Keith McGowan	Stephen Bently-Klein	William Lyons	Leon Scott

exam PREPARATION

You will answer two questions on *Romeo and Juliet* in your exam. Marks are given for how well you do against the Assessment Objectives. Note that not every Assessment Objective is assessed for every question in the exam. Below is a summary of which ones apply to you when you are examined on *Romeo and Juliet*.

(AO1) Response to characters and events

- write about your personal response to aspects of plot, characterisation, events and settings
- comment in detail on characters' motivation, the sequence of events, and links between events
- support your point of view by referring to and quoting from the text.

(AO2) Language, structure and form

- write in detail about the language Shakespeare uses, using appropriate linguistic and literary terminology
- show your understanding of techniques by explaining their effects.

(AO4) Vocabulary, sentence structure and spelling

- use a range of vocabulary and sentence structures for clarity, purpose and effect, with accurate spelling and punctuation.

Question format

- An extract from *Romeo and Juliet* with one question worth 15 marks. (Assesses AO1/AO2.)
- An essay question on *Romeo and Juliet* worth 25 marks. (Assesses AO1/AO2/AO4.)

Example:

Romeo and Juliet
Answer **both** part (a) **and** part (b). You are advised to spend about 20 minutes on part (a), and about 40 minutes on part (b).

(a) Read the extract.
How does Shakespeare present mood and atmosphere for an audience here? Refer closely to details from the extract to support your answer.   [15]

(b) How is Mercutio important to the play as a whole?   [25]
(Five of this question's marks are allocated for accuracy in spelling, punctuation and the use of vocabulary and sentence structures.)

Note that the following approaches are not the only way of answering questions but are offered as possible ways of meeting the demands of the exam extract and essay.

How to respond to an extract question

20 minutes. 15 marks. AO1, AO2.

- Spend about 5 minutes reading the extract and the question carefully. Underline or highlight the key words in the question and the bullet points.

- You don't need an introduction, but should say where in the play the extract comes from. You don't need to state which act and scene (although you can state this if you know). Rather, say what has happened just before this extract or, briefly, what is happening in it, so that you put the extract in place, for example: *"This is taken from Act 3, just after the Nurse has brought news of Tybalt's death. In this scene, Juliet initially misinterprets the Nurse's words and believes that Romeo has been killed."*

- Ensure that you are addressing the demands of the question exactly. If you are asked to explore mood and atmosphere, you must state what the mood is, such as, *"This creates a frightening mood,"* *"This creates a tense atmosphere."* Never just write *"This creates mood."* There must be an adjective, stating what mood is being created. Also be aware that the mood may not be constant throughout the extract. In the question "How does the character of…speak and behave here?", you will need to say, *"He speaks angrily when…"*, *"She behaves in a frightened manner when…"*

- Use a **P**oint-**E**vidence-**E**xplanation structure and include a spread of points from across the extract. Make a **p**oint – find supporting **e**vidence – then explain its **e**ffect. For example: **[point]** *Shakespeare uses imagery to convey Romeo's state of mind when he first meets Juliet.* **[evidence]** *Comparing her to "This holy shrine" and his lips to, "two blushing pilgrims".* **[explain]** *shows just how wonderful he thinks she is.*

- One-word quotes are especially productive. They show close attention to language. As well as longer quotes, try to pick out and analyse about three one-word quotes across your extract.

- Try to link one of your points to a wider theme in the play, such as, "The theme of fate is presented when…" This shows the examiner that you have an overview of how the extract fits into the play as a whole.

Practice

Read Act 1 scene 5 lines 73-110.

How does Shakespeare present mood and atmosphere in this scene? [15]

Note: guidelines for this question appear on page 33.

Use the checklist at the end of this section to assess your response.

How to respond to an essay question

40 minutes. 25 marks. AO1, AO2, AO4.

- You should have a brief plan, either written down or in your head, of how the essay will unfold. For a character essay, this can be:

- introduction
- when we first meet the character
- personal qualities
- main events
- conclusion.

- For a theme essay, your plan might list the characters who are linked to this theme. For love:
  - Romeo and Juliet
  - Rosaline
  - Paris

  and you may also wish to reference others who show other kinds of love, such as parental love (or lack of it) from the Capulets, Montagues, the Nurse and the Friar. You could also include love through friendship here.
- Your brief introduction should engage with the question immediately.
- Avoid re-telling the story. Events need a brief recap on which to build your point, but you should use **P**oint-**E**vidence-**E**xplanation throughout.
- Try learning a few short quotes, such as Romeo is first "gentle" in Act 1, then "pale and wild" in Act 5. Capulet believes Juliet to be "ruled / In all respects" by him, then calls her "baggage" in Act 3. This cross-reference shows that you know the play well.

Practice

(b) How is Mercutio important to the play as a whole? (25 marks)
5 of this question's marks are allocated for spelling, punctuation, vocabulary and sentence structures.

Guideline plan

The following plan uses a basic outline and adds detail specific to the question above.
- *Introduction* – overview of importance of character.
- When we first meet the character – 1.4. He is brash and humorous: a foil (opposite) to Romeo's romantic nature. Contrast to Benvolio's reasonable character. Queen Mab speech. Full of puns and vivid imagery. Importance? – mocks the nature of love. Romeo seems a serious man by contrast.
- *Personal qualities* – Can be mocking; cynical; loyal; antagonistic. *Find evidence of each.*
- *Main events* –
  - *2.1* – loses Romeo after the ball. Importance? Demonstrates how secret the meeting was.
  - *2.4* – Bawdy conversation with Romeo. Teases the Nurse.
  - Romeo does not confide in Mercutio about Juliet. Importance? Shows danger of telling others about Juliet.
  - 3.1 – Mercutio is "apt to quarrel" and challenges Tybalt by inviting "a word and a blow." Argumentative. Fight scene.

- Mercutio injured. Jokes initially. Different side of character shown when extent of injury is realised – "A plague o' both your houses!" Dies. "brave Mercutio," "gallant spirit." Importance? Shows the feud permeates everywhere. Also makes Mercutio a plot vehicle – Romeo fights – Tybalt dies – Romeo banished.
- *Conclusion* – Presents a different view of love. Something fun and not to be taken too seriously. Plot vehicle. Death marks a turning-point in the play – becomes tragic.

(AO4) Vocabulary, sentence structure and spelling

Avoid slang in your answer. Vary your expression: *This illustrates / conveys / portrays.*
Learn some impressive vocabulary: *bawdy, cynical, eloquent, scornful, irascible, antagonistic.*

Example:
Introduction

The character of Mercutio is presented as a foil for Romeo's romantic nature. His humorous speeches lift the serious mood of the play and he serves as a vehicle for the plot when his death is the cause of Romeo's banishment and ultimately, the play's tragic conclusion.

When we first meet the characters

The audience already knows Romeo's friend, Benvolio; a thoughtful character who makes several attempts to keep peace in Verona. By contrast, Mercutio is a witty, carefree man, shown by his dismissal of anyone who criticises him, claiming,

"What care I
What curious eye doth quote deformities?"

showing his cavalier attitude.

He is wildly imaginative and mocks Romeo freely.

Now continue this response.

Checklist

Check your answers against the ascending skills on this list:
- uses **P**oint-**E**vidence-**E**xplanation
- **P**oint-**E**vidence-**E**xplanation is thoughtful
- thorough coverage of the extract / play
- explores language, techniques and effects
- specific analysis of language, techniques and effects
- assured, sensitive discussion
- evaluates (assesses) language and techniques
- perceptive, often sophisticated points.

ACT 1 SCENE 1

THE PROLOGUE

Enter Chorus.

Chorus   Two households, both alike in dignity,
(In fair Verona, where we lay our scene),
From ancient grudge break to new mutiny,
Where civil blood makes civil hands unclean.
From forth the fatal loins of these two foes   5
A pair of star-crossed lovers take their life,
Whose misadventured piteous overthrows
Doth with their death bury their parents' strife.
The fearful passage of their death-marked love,
And the continuance of their parents' rage   10
(Which but their children's end, nought could remove),
Is now the two hours' traffic of our stage.
The which if you with patient ears attend,
What here shall miss, our toil shall strive to mend.

Exit.

ACT 1 SCENE 1

Enter Sampson and Gregory, of the house of Capulet, armed with swords and bucklers.

Sampson   Gregory, on my word we'll not carry coals.

Gregory   No, for then we should be colliers.

Sampson   I mean, if we be in choler, we'll draw.

Gregory   Ay, while you live, draw your neck out o' the collar.

Sampson   I strike quickly, being moved.   5

Gregory   But thou art not quickly moved to strike.

Sampson   A dog of the house of Montague moves me.

Gregory   To move is to stir; and to be valiant is to stand.
Therefore, if thou art moved, thou runn'st away.

Sampson   A dog of that house shall move me to stand. I will take   10
the wall of any man or maid of Montague's.

Gregory   That shows thee a weak slave, for the weakest goes to
the wall.

Sampson   'Tis true, and therefore women being the weaker
vessels are ever thrust to the wall. Therefore I will push   15
Montague's men from the wall, and thrust his maids to
the wall.

Gregory   The quarrel is between our masters and us, their men.

Sampson   'Tis all one. I will show myself a tyrant. When I have
fought with the men, I will be civil with the maids, I   20
will cut off their heads.

Gregory   The heads of the maids?

---

1   **dignity:** social status
3   **ancient grudge:** old quarrels
3   **break to new mutiny:** begin new quarrel
4   **Where civil blood ... hands unclean:** fighting and spilling blood even though they are not soldiers at war
5   **From forth the fatal loins ... two foes:** from these two warring households
6   **star-crossed:** doomed by fate
7   **misadventured piteous overthows:** tragic, steps to ruin
11   **but:** except
11   **nought:** nothing
12   **traffic of our stage:** subject of our play
14   **What here shall miss ... to mend:** We'll work hard to tell you the full story

SD   **bucklers:** small, round shields

1   **carry coals:** be insulted
2   **colliers:** coal sellers
3   **be in choler:** are angry
3   **draw:** draw our swords
4   **collar:** hangman's rope (wordplay uses collier/choler/collar which sound similar)
5   **being moved:** if I'm made angry

8   **stir:** run away
8   **stand:** stay and fight

10-1   **take the wall:** walk by the wall (the best part of the street) furthest from the centre of the street where the gutter was
12   **slave:** used to show contempt (he thinks Sampson is boasting)
12-3   **the weakest goes to the wall:** from a proverb meaning the weakest must give in
14-5   **weaker vessels:** naturally weaker than men

19   **'Tis all one:** it makes no difference

THE PROLOGUE

The Prologue is in the form of a 14-line sonnet. In seven groups, each group is given a different couplet from the Prologue.

- Identify the key words and images in your couplet.
- Create a freeze frame to illustrate the essence of your couplet.
- Now, speak the whole line, emphasising the key words you identified.
- In sequence, the whole class creates the Prologue by performing their couplets in the right order. Watch and listen.

1 Which words and phrases create vivid images in your mind?

2 What does the Prologue tell us about what will happen in the play?

3 The Prologue reveals the ending at the start.

   a) How might this affect an audience's view of the "star-crossed lovers" and their parents?

   b) Why might Shakespeare have chosen to remind his audience with "the two hours' traffic of the stage" that theatre is illusion?

Sampson	Ay, the heads of the maids, or their maidenheads, take it in what sense thou wilt.	23 **maidenheads:** virginities
Gregory	They must take it in sense, that feel it.	25 **They must take ... feel it:** it isn't me that has to take it, but the maids
Sampson	Me they shall feel while I am able to stand, and 'tis known I am a pretty piece of flesh.	27 **a pretty piece of flesh:** a fine figure of a man (this starts a series of sexual double meanings)
Gregory	'Tis well thou art not fish. If thou hadst, thou hadst been poor John. — Draw thy tool, here comes two of the house of the Montagues.	29 **poor John:** salted and dried cheap fish mostly eaten by the poor
		29 **tool:** sword
	Enter Abraham and Balthasar, serving men of the Montagues.	31 **My naked weapon is out:** my sword is out of my scabbard
		31 **Quarrel:** start a fight
Sampson	My naked weapon is out. Quarrel, I will back thee.	
Gregory	How? Turn thy back and run?	
Sampson	Fear me not.	33 **Fear me not:** Don't worry that I'll run
Gregory	No, marry, I fear thee.	
Sampson	Let us take the law of our sides. Let them begin.	35 **take the law of our sides:** seem to be keeping the law
Gregory	I will frown as I pass by, and let them take it as they list.	36 **as they list:** however they want
Sampson	Nay, as they dare. I will bite my thumb at them; which is a disgrace to them, if they bear it.	37 **bite my thumb:** an insulting gesture at the time
Abraham	Do you bite your thumb at us, sir?	
Sampson	I do bite my thumb, sir.	
Abraham	Do you bite your thumb at us, sir?	
Sampson	*[Aside to Gregory.]* Is the law of our side, if I say 'ay'?	
Gregory	*[Aside to Sampson.]* No.	
Sampson	No, sir, I do not bite my thumb at you, sir. But I bite my thumb, sir.	

Line numbers: 25, 30, 35, 40, 45

Capulet (left) and Montague in the foreground while their retainers fight behind them, 2013.

1 Why must this photo have been taken after line 73? Give reasons for your answer.

2 On the evidence of the first scene, why might a director choose to set the play in modern dress?

Jason Baughan, Dickon Tyrrell

Gregory	Do you quarrel, sir?
Abraham	Quarrel, sir? No, sir.
Sampson	If you do, sir, I am for you. I serve as good a man as you.
Abraham	No better?
Sampson	Well, sir —
Gregory	Say "better": here comes one of my master's kinsmen.
Sampson	Yes, better, sir.
Abraham	You lie.
Sampson	Draw if you be men. Gregory, remember thy washing blow.

They fight.

Benvolio	Part, fools! Put up your swords, you know not what you do.

Enter Tybalt.

Tybalt	What, art thou drawn among these heartless hinds? Turn thee, Benvolio, look upon thy death.
Benvolio	I do but keep the peace, put up thy sword, Or manage it to part these men with me.
Tybalt	What, drawn, and talk of peace? I hate the word, As I hate hell, all Montagues, and thee. Have at thee, coward! *They fight.*

Enter several Montagues and Capulets who join in the fight, also an officer and three of four citizens with clubs or partisans.

48 **I am for you:** I'll fight you

50

55

55 **washing:** slashing

58 **Put up:** put away

59 **heartless hinds:** cowardly servants (double meaning of female deer without a male for protection)
61 **I do but keep the peace:** I'm just trying to stop this fighting
62 **manage it:** use it

60

65

10

Officer   Clubs, bills, and partisans! Strike! Beat them down!
Down with the Capulets! Down with the Montagues!

Enter Capulet in his gown, and Lady Capulet.

Capulet   What noise is this? Give me my long sword, ho!

Lady Capulet   A crutch, a crutch! Why call you for a sword?

Capulet   My sword, I say! Old Montague is come,   70
And flourishes his blade in spite of me.

Enter Montague and Lady Montague.

Montague   Thou villain Capulet. — Hold me not, let me go.

Lady Montague   Thou shalt not stir one foot to seek a foe.

Enter Prince Escalus, with his Attendants.

Prince   Rebellious subjects, enemies to peace,
Profaners of this neighbour-stainèd steel, —   75
Will they not hear? What, ho! you men, you beasts,
That quench the fire of your pernicious rage
With purple fountains issuing from your veins.
On pain of torture, from those bloody hands
Throw your mistempered weapons to the ground,   80
And hear the sentence of your movèd Prince.
Three civil brawls, bred of an airy word,
By thee, old Capulet, and Montague,
Have thrice disturbed the quiet of our streets,
And made Verona's ancient citizens   85
Cast by their grave beseeming ornaments,
To wield old partisans, in hands as old,
Cankered with peace, to part your cankered hate.
If ever you disturb our streets again,
Your lives shall pay the forfeit of the peace.   90
For this time all the rest depart away.
You, Capulet, shall go along with me,
And Montague, come you this afternoon,
To know our further pleasure in this case,
To old Free-town, our common judgement-place.   95
Once more, on pain of death, all men depart.

Exit all but Montague, Lady Montague, and Benvolio.

---

66 **bills, and partisans:** types of spear

68 **long sword:** old-fashioned heavy sword
69 **A crutch, a crutch!:** she's suggesting it's too heavy for an old man like him to lift, he might as well lean on it, like a crutch
71 **in spite of me:** scornfully, to provoke me

75 **Profaners of this neighbour-stainèd steel:** who have shown contempt for my orders and God by fighting and wounding fellow citizens
77 **quench:** put out
77 **pernicious:** harmful, destructive
79 **On pain of torture:** unless you want to be tortured as a punishment
80 **mistempered:** used with a double meaning of 'badly made' (for swords) and 'angry' for the people using them
81 **sentence:** punishment
81 **movèd:** angry
82 **civil brawls:** outbreaks of fighting between citizens
82 **bred of an airy word:** over some trivial remark
86-7 **Cast by their grave ... wield old partisans:** give up the sensible pursuits of old age and take up their old weapons to fight
88 **Cankered with peace:** rusty through disuse in times of peace
88 **cankered hate:** festering hate
90 **Your lives shall pay the forfeit of the peace:** you'll be executed
94 **our further pleasure:** what else I decide to do

---

exam SKILLS

Target skill: analysing language

Question: Explore how the Prince is presented through his speech in lines 74–96.

Prince Escalus is concerned about maintaining peace. The "ancient quarrel" between Montagues and Capulets threatens the social order.

1 The Prince's serious nature is shown through his language. What negative images does he use to describe the feuding sides? Start with "neighbour-stainèd steel"; take two of the images and discuss them with a partner – what could they mean?

2 Decide what the Prince's state of mind is in this extract. Find evidence to support your opinion.

3 What is the Prince's opinion of the feud? Find evidence to support your points.

ACT 1 SCENE 1

Montague	Who set this ancient quarrel new abroach?
	Speak, nephew, were you by when it began?
Benvolio	Here were the servants of your adversary,
	And yours, close fighting ere I did approach.
	I drew to part them. In the instant came
	The fiery Tybalt, with his sword prepared,
	Which, as he breathed defiance to my ears,
	He swung about his head and cut the winds,
	Who nothing hurt withal, hissed him in scorn.
	While we were interchanging thrusts and blows,
	Came more and more, and fought on part and part,
	Till the Prince came, who parted either part.
Lady Montague	O, where is Romeo, saw you him to-day?
	Right glad I am he was not at this fray.
Benvolio	Madam, an hour before the worshipped sun
	Peered forth the golden window of the east,
	A troubled mind drove me to walk abroad,
	Where, underneath the grove of sycamore
	That westward rooteth from the city side,
	So early walking did I see your son.
	Towards him I made, but he was ware of me
	And stole into the covert of the wood.
	I, measuring his affections by my own,
	Which then most sought where most might not be found,
	Being one too many by my weary self,
	That most are busied when they're most alone,
	Pursued my humour not pursuing his,
	And gladly shunned who gladly fled from me.
Montague	Many a morning hath he there been seen,
	With tears augmenting the fresh morning's dew,
	Adding to clouds more clouds with his deep sighs.

97 **set this ancient quarrel new abroach:** started this old quarrel up again

98 **by:** nearby

99 **adversary:** enemy

100 **ere:** before

105 **Who nothing hurt withal:** which, unharmed

107 **Came more and more:** more and more people arrived

107 **on part and part:** on one side or the other

108 **either part:** them both

110 **Right glad I am he was not at this fray:** I'm very glad he wasn't part of this fight

115 **rooteth:** grow

117 **made:** went

117 **he was ware of me:** he noticed me

118 **covert:** shelter

120 **most sought where most might not be found:** wanted most to be by myself

121–2 **Being one too many ... they're most alone:** even my own company was too much for me, my mind was so busy

123–4 **Pursued my humour ... fled from me:** did what I wanted most and avoided him as he avoided me

126 **augmenting:** adding to

---

exam SKILLS

Target skill: analysing a character

You need to be prepared for questions on character. An extract question might ask you:

- Look at how the characters speak and behave here. How do you think an audience might respond to this part of the play?

or

- How is the character of…presented in this extract?

An essay question might ask you:

- How is the character of…important to the play as a whole?

or

- Write about the character of…and the way he/she is presented in the play.

Question: How does Shakespeare influence the audience's first impressions of Romeo?

Use lines 97–139, 140–177, 177–202 and 203–232.

1 Highlight the words or phrases that tell you something about Romeo.

2 Organise them into lists to illustrate:
 - what Romeo's parents say about him
 - what Romeo's friend says about him
 - what Romeo says about himself.

3 What do the lists tell us about Romeo's personality and character? Support your opinion with evidence.

4 What is Romeo's view of love and being in love?

But all so soon as the all-cheering sun
Should in the furthest east begin to draw
The shady curtains from Aurora's bed,
Away from light steals home my heavy son,
And private in his chamber pens himself,
Shuts up his windows, locks fair daylight out
And makes himself an artificial night.
Black and portentous must this humour prove,
Unless good counsel may the cause remove.

Benvolio   My noble uncle, do you know the cause?

Montague   I neither know it, nor can learn of him.

Benvolio   Have you importuned him by any means?

Montague   Both by myself and many other friends.
But he, his own affections' counsellor,
Is to himself, (I will not say how true)
But to himself so secret and so close,
So far from sounding and discovery,
As is the bud bit with an envious worm,
Ere he can spread his sweet leaves to the air,
Or dedicate his beauty to the same.
Could we but learn from whence his sorrows grow.
We would as willingly give cure as know.

Enter Romeo.

Benvolio   See, where he comes. So please you step aside,
I'll know his grievance, or be much denied.

Montague   I would thou wert so happy by thy stay,
To hear true shrift. Come madam, let's away.

Exit Montague and Lady Montague.

Benvolio   Good morrow, cousin.

Romeo   Is the day so young?

Benvolio   But new struck nine.

Romeo   Ay me, sad hours seem long.
Was that my father that went hence so fast?

Benvolio   It was. What sadness lengthens Romeo's hours?

Romeo   Not having that, which having, makes them short.

Benvolio   In love?

Romeo   Out —

Benvolio   Of love?

Romeo   Out of her favour, where I am in love.

Benvolio   Alas that love, so gentle in his view,
Should be so tyrannous and rough in proof!

Romeo   Alas, that love, whose view is muffled still,
Should without eyes see pathways to his will. —
Where shall we dine? — O me! What fray was here?

130
131
132
135
135

136
139

139
141

142
144
145
148

149

150

151

152–3

154
154

156

162

163

160 163

164

165

165 166

130 **Aurora:** goddess of the dawn (both Benvolio and Montague give very flowery description of dawn)
131 **heavy:** sad
132 **pens himself:** shuts himself up
135 **Black:** gloomy
135 **portentous:** suggesting future misfortune
135 **humour:** mood (also refers to the 'Four Humours' medical theory used at the time where too much of one 'humour' in the body was said to cause illness. Too much black bile caused depression)
136 **counsel:** advice
139 **importuned:** pressed him to tell you
139 **by any means:** in any way
141 **his own affections' counsellor:** is the only person he'll share his feelings with
142 **true:** trustworthy
144 **sounding:** being easy to question
145 **envious worm:** the canker worm that eats through flower buds
148 **from whence his sorrows grow:** what is making him so unhappy
149 **We would as willingly give cure as know:** we want to help as much as we want to know the problem
150 **So please you:** please
151 **his grievance, or be much denied:** what's upsetting him, I won't take no for an answer
152–3 **I would thou wert so happy ... true shrift:** I hope you can get him to tell you the truth (shrift means confessing to a priest)
154 **morrow:** morning
154 **cousin:** used to close relatives and friends
156 **hence:** away from here

162 **Out of her favour:** no longer loved
163 **so gentle in his view:** so attractive as an idea
164 **be so tyrannous and rough in proof:** treat us so badly when we experience it
165 **whose view is muffled still:** refers to the fact that Cupid, the god of love, was said to be blind or blindfolded
166 **see pathways to his will:** still be able to make what he wants happen

13

SHAKESPEARE'S WORLD
◇◇◇◇◇◇◇◇◇◇◇◇

Elizabethan view of romantic love

In this scene, Benvolio and Romeo discuss how love can make a man act like a madman. Elizabethans had complicated ideas about romantic love. People were encouraged to love their husband or wife. However, loving someone too much was seen as an illness. Elizabethan doctors saw unrequited love or desire as a disease, a type of melancholy sometimes called lovesickness. It was caught through the eye. Symptoms of lovesickness were: fever, mood swings and even shrinking of the heart. Medical writings treated lovesickness as a common disease. Doctors tried various cures. They changed the patient's diet, and gave them herbal medicines. They sometimes sent patients to church, to confess to a priest. They believed that, if lovesickness was left untreated, it could lead to madness.

The lovesick man was a popular character in early modern literature. Shakespeare makes the connection between love and madness again in *Hamlet*, when Polonius believes Hamlet to be mad because of his love for Ophelia.

exam SKILLS

Target skill: analysing imagery

Question: How does Shakespeare present the idea of love in lines 165–193?

Love is a major theme in the play. Look first at the Shakespeare's World section on the Elizabethan view of romantic love.

In *Romeo and Juliet* Shakespeare showed his original audience that he knew about the literary tradition of courtly love, in which the male (young and usually noble) worships the lady (beautiful, chaste and usually unattainable) with an unrequited passion that is spiritual rather than physical.

- Working in threes, read aloud lines 165–190, changing reader at every punctuation mark. List or highlight all the images you noticed during your reading. Identify at least 15 different ways in which Shakespeare has Romeo describe love.
- List the things that are compared to love. Each individual should choose the three that they find most striking and discuss what gives them their impact.

Compare your choices with other people's.
- Many of the phrases you found, for example "heavy lightness", are *oxymorons* – a figure of speech in which apparent opposites appear together. What might Shakespeare be suggesting about Romeo's feelings and the nature of love by using oxymorons to link things that are usually opposites?

1 In your group, find a quote that supports each of the following statements:
   a) Shakespeare is suggesting that love is complex and full of contradictions.
   b) Shakespeare is suggesting that love has physical effects.
   c) Love makes you feel like you are not yourself.
2 Shakespeare structures this scene by having Romeo speaking at length about love in general, and only mentioning Rosaline herself towards the end of the scene. What do you think this tells you about Romeo's love of Rosaline?
3 How does thinking about the images Shakespeare has Romeo use help you answer the question above?

Yet tell me not, for I have heard it all.
Here's much to do with hate, but more with love.
Why, then, O brawling love, O loving hate,   170
O any thing, of nothing first created.
O heavy lightness, serious vanity,
Misshapen chaos of well-seeming forms,
Feather of lead, bright smoke, cold fire, sick health,   175
Still-waking sleep, that is not what it is.
This love feel I, that feel no love in this.
Dost thou not laugh?

Benvolio   No, coz, I rather weep.

Romeo   Good heart, at what?

Benvolio   At thy good heart's oppression.

Romeo   Why such is love's transgression.   180
Griefs of mine own lie heavy in my breast,
Which thou wilt propagate, to have it pressed
With more of thine. This love that thou hast shown
Doth add more grief to too much of mine own.
Love is a smoke made with the fume of sighs,   185
Being purged, a fire sparkling in lovers' eyes,
Being vex'd a sea nourish'd with loving tears.
What is it else? A madness most discreet,
A choking gall and a preserving sweet.
Farewell, my coz.

Benvolio   Soft! I will go along,   190
And if you leave me so, you do me wrong.

Romeo   Tut, I have lost myself, I am not here,
This is not Romeo, he's some other where.

Benvolio   Tell me in sadness, who is that you love?

Romeo   What, shall I groan and tell thee?   195

Benvolio   Groan? Why, no. But sadly tell me who.

Romeo   Bid a sick man in sadness make his will.
A word ill urged to one that is so ill.
In sadness, cousin, I do love a woman.

Benvolio   I aimed so near when I supposed you loved.   200

Romeo   A right good mark-man, and she's fair I love.

Benvolio   A right fair mark, fair coz, is soonest hit.

Romeo   Well, in that hit you miss, she'll not be hit
With Cupid's arrow. She hath Dian's wit.
And, in strong proof of chastity well armed,   205
From love's weak childish bow she lives uncharmed.
She will not stay the siege of loving terms,
Nor bide th' encounter of assailing eyes,
Nor ope her lap to saint-seducing gold.
O she is rich in beauty, only poor   210
That when she dies, with beauty dies her store.

171 of nothing first created: made out of nothing in the first place
172 O heavy lightness ... : the start of a sequence of pairings of opposites
173 well-seeming forms: attractive looking shapes
175 Still-waking: not sleeping
176 This love feel I ... no love in this: I love, but am not loved in return
177 coz: cousin
177 rather weep: weep instead
179 oppression: heaviness, misery
180 love's transgression: the way love steps outside its proper limits
182 pressed: burdened
186 purged: cleaned, purified
188 discreet: cautious, prudent
189 choking gall: a bitter liquid that chokes you
189 preserving sweet: a sweet, healing liquid
190 Soft!: wait!
194 in sadness: in all seriousness
200 I aimed so near ... you loved: I'd worked that out when I guessed you were in love
201 A right good mark-man: an excellent guess
202 A right fair mark: an easy target
204 Dian's wit: the skills of Diana, the goddess of chastity
205 proof: armour
206 From love's weak childish bow she lives uncharmed: she's unaffected by Cupid's arrows
207-8 stay the siege of loving terms ... assailing eyes: listen to a lover's words or even let him gaze adoringly
209 Nor ope her lap to saint-seducing gold: you can't buy her love, either
211 her store: the virginity she's been saving

Benvolio	Then she hath sworn that she will still live chaste?
Romeo	She hath, and in that sparing makes huge waste,
	For beauty starved with her severity
	Cuts beauty off from all posterity.
	She is too fair, too wise, wisely too fair,
	To merit bliss by making me despair.
	She hath forsworn to love, and in that vow
	Do I live dead, that live to tell it now.
Benvolio	Be ruled by me, forget to think of her.
Romeo	O teach me how I should forget to think.
Benvolio	By giving liberty unto thine eyes,
	Examine other beauties.
Romeo	'Tis the way
	To call hers, exquisite, in question more.
	These happy masks that kiss fair ladies' brows,
	Being black, put us in mind they hide the fair.
	He that is strucken blind cannot forget
	The precious treasure of his eyesight lost.
	Show me a mistress that is passing fair.
	What doth her beauty serve but as a note,
	Where I may read who passed that passing fair?
	Farewell, thou canst not teach me to forget.
Benvolio	I'll pay that doctrine, or else die in debt. *They exit.*

ACT 1 SCENE 2

Enter Capulet, Paris and Peter.

Capulet	But Montague is bound as well as I,
	In penalty alike, and 'tis not hard I think,
	For men so old as we to keep the peace.
Paris	Of honourable reckoning are you both,
	And pity 'tis you lived at odds so long.
	But now, my lord, what say you to my suit?
Capulet	But saying o'er what I have said before.
	My child is yet a stranger in the world,
	She hath not seen the change of fourteen years,
	Let two more summers wither in their pride,
	Ere we may think her ripe to be a bride.
Paris	Younger than she are happy mothers made.
Capulet	And too soon marred are those so early made.
	The earth hath swallowed all my hopes but she,
	She is the hopeful lady of my earth.
	But woo her, gentle Paris, get her heart,
	My will to her consent is but a part.
	And she agreed, within her scope of choice
	Lies my consent and fair according voice.
	This night I hold an old accustomed feast,
	Whereto I have invited many a guest,

213 **sparing:** saving, hoarding up
215 **Cuts beauty off from all posterity:** will not have children as beautiful as she is
217 **To merit bliss by making me despair:** to earn happiness in heaven through her chastity by making me miserable now
218 **forsworn to:** sworn not to
219 **live dead:** I might as well be dead
223-4 **'Tis the way … question more:** that will just confirm her beauty
225 **happy:** lucky
231 **Where I may read … passing fair:** that reminds me my love is more beautiful
233 **I'll pay that doctrine … in debt:** I will teach you that or die trying

Director's Note, 1.1

✔ Servants of the Montagues and Capulets start a street fight.
✔ The Prince stops the fight, and threatens any more fighting will be punished by death.
✔ Montague is worried about Romeo's behaviour. Benvolio agrees to question him.
✔ Romeo admits he is in love, but the woman he loves is not interested in him.
✔ What might the audience expect will happen next to Romeo?

1 **bound:** ordered to keep the peace
2 **In penalty alike:** with the same punishment for failing
4 **reckoning:** reputation
6 **suit:** request
7 **But:** nothing more than
8 **yet a stranger in the world:** very young
11 **Ere:** before
12 **Younger than she are happy mothers made:** younger girls are married with children
13 **too soon marred …. early made:** they are spoiled by it
14 **The earth hath swallowed … but she:** all my other children are dead
15 **the hopeful lady of my earth:** she's my only child and will inherit my wealth
17 **My will to her consent is but a part:** she has to agree as well
18-9 **And she agreed … according voice:** and I'll accept any suitable person she chooses
20 **old accustomed:** traditional
21 **Whereto:** to which

Romeo and Peter, summer 2009.

This photograph was taken during the text on pages 17 and 18. Pick a line which you think was the one being spoken when the photo was taken. Give reasons for your answer.

Adetomiwa Edun, Fergal McElherron

SHAKESPEARE'S WORLD

Peter and Will Kemp

In two of the versions of *Romeo and Juliet* printed during Shakespeare's lifetime, the name 'Peter' is replaced in a stage direction by 'Will Kemp'. Peter, the Capulets' servant, is fictional. Kemp was real – he was the actor who first played the part of Peter. Kemp was a celebrity in Elizabethan London, and one of the star attractions of the Chamberlain's Men, the company Shakespeare was part of. Audiences came to watch him for two things: clowning and dancing.

Peter is the clown of *Romeo and Juliet*. It may seem as though he does not have many lines, especially when he was one of the stars the audiences went to see. But clowns often said more than the author wrote, and the crowd enjoyed the sharp wit of celebrated comedians. So, with Kemp playing the part, he probably said much more, and it would have been new every time. Even if he didn't spend much time on the stage during the play, Kemp certainly dominated it afterwards. Every play, whether it was a comedy, tragedy or history, would finish with a jig – a dance, often with a comic song. Kemp was an undisputed master of this part of the performance and his jigs were every bit as famous, and as popular, as Shakespeare's plays.

Such as I love, and you among the store,
One more, most welcome, makes my number more.
At my poor house look to behold this night
Earth-treading stars that make dark heaven light. 25
Such comfort as do lusty young men feel,
When well-apparelled April on the heel
Of limping winter treads, even such delight
Among fresh fennel buds shall you this night
Inherit at my house. Hear all, all see, 30
And like her most whose merit most shall be.
Which on more view, of many, mine being one,
May stand in number, though in reckoning none.
Come, go with me.   *[To Peter, giving him a paper.]*
                    Go, sirrah, trudge about
Through fair Verona, find those persons out 35
Whose names are written there, and to them say,
My house and welcome on their pleasure stay.

Exit Capulet and Paris.

Peter   Find them out whose names are written here.
It is written, that the shoemaker should meddle with
his yard, and the tailor with his last, the fisher with 40
his pencil, and the painter with his nets. But I am
sent to find those persons whose names are here
writ, and can never find what names the writing
person hath here writ. I must to the learnèd. —
In good time. 45

22 **the store:** them

25 **Earth-treading stars:** many beautiful women

27 **well-apparelled:** beautifully dressed

29 **fennel:** a herb linked at the time to passion

30 **Inherit at:** be free to enjoy

31 **like her most whose merit most shall be:** see who you think is the most desirable

32 **mine:** my daughter

33 **May stand in number ... reckoning none:** may be one of them, although not among the most well-known beauties

34 **sirrah:** you, used to call a less important person

37 **stay:** wait

39 **meddle with:** busy himself with

40 **yard:** measuring stick used by a tailor (he confuses the various pieces of equipment and trades)

40 **last:** wooden foot used to measure shoes

43-4 **can never find ... hath here writ:** can't read

ACT 1 SCENE 2

Enter Benvolio and Romeo, talking.

Benvolio	Tut, man, one fire burns out another's burning,
	One pain is lessened by another's anguish.
	Turn giddy, and be helped by backward turning.
	One desperate grief cures with another's languish.
	Take thou some new infection to thy eye, 50
	And the rank poison of the old will die.
Romeo	Your plantain leaf is excellent for that.
Benvolio	For what, I pray thee?
Romeo	For your broken shin.
Benvolio	Why, Romeo, art thou mad?
Romeo	Not mad, but bound more than a mad-man is: 55
	Shut up in prison, kept without my food,
	Whipped and tormented and—Good-e'en, good fellow.
Peter	God gi' good-e'en. I pray, sir, can you read?
Romeo	Ay, mine own fortune in my misery.
Peter	Perhaps you have learned it without book. But I pray, 60
	can you read anything you see?
Romeo	Ay, if I know the letters and the language.
Peter	Ye say honestly, rest you merry!
Romeo	Stay, fellow; I can read. *He reads the letter.*
	Signior Martino and his wife and daughters; County 65
	Anselme and his beauteous sisters; the lady widow of
	Vitravio; Signior Placentio and his lovely nieces; Mercutio
	and his brother Valentine; mine uncle Capulet, his wife and
	daughters; my fair niece Rosaline; Livia; Signior Valentio
	and his cousin Tybalt; Lucio and the lively Helena. 70
	A fair assembly: whither should they come?
Peter	Up.
Romeo	Whither? To supper?
Peter	To our house.
Romeo	Whose house? 75
Peter	My master's.
Romeo	Indeed I should have asked you that before.
Peter	Now I'll tell you without asking. my master is the
	great rich Capulet, and if you be not of the house of
	Montagues, I pray, come and crush a cup of wine. Rest 80
	you merry! *Exit Peter.*
Benvolio	At this same ancient feast of Capulet's
	Sups the fair Rosaline, whom thou so loves,
	With all the admired beauties of Verona.
	Go thither and with unattainted eye, 85
	Compare her face with some that I shall show,
	And I will make thee think thy swan a crow.

47 **another's anguish:** the pain that was there before
48 **backward turning:** turning the other way
49 **cures with another's languish:** is cured by the arrival of another
50 **Take thou some new infection to thy eye:** fall in love with someone else
51 **rank:** strong
52 **plantain leaf:** used to heal cuts

57 **Good-e'en:** a greeting used after midday
58 **gi':** give you

60 **without book:** off by heart

63 **rest you merry:** farewell

65 **County:** Count

71 **whither should they come?:** where are they invited?

80 **crush:** drink

83 **Sups:** has her supper

85 **thither:** there
85 **unattainted:** unprejudiced

Romeo	When the devout religion of mine eye Maintains such falsehood, then turn tears to fire, And these who often drowned could never die, 90 Transparent heretics, be burnt for liars. One fairer than my love? The all-seeing sun Ne'er saw her match since first the world begun.
Benvolio	Tut, you saw her fair, none else being by, Herself poised with herself in either eye. 95 But in that crystal scales let there be weighed Your lady's love against some other maid That I will show you shining at this feast, And she shall scant show well that now seems best.
Romeo	I'll go along, no such sight to be shown, 100 But to rejoice in splendour of mine own. *Exit both.*

ACT 1 SCENE 3

Enter Lady Capulet and Nurse.

Lady Capulet	Nurse, where's my daughter? call her forth to me.
Nurse	Now, by my maidenhead at twelve year old I bade her come. What, lamb! What, ladybird! God forbid, where's this girl? What, Juliet!

Enter Juliet.

Juliet	How now, who calls? 5
Nurse	Your mother.
Juliet	Madam, I am here. What is your will?
Lady Capulet	This is the matter. — Nurse, give leave awhile, We must talk in secret. — Nurse, come back again, I have remembered me, thou's hear our counsel. 10 Thou knowest my daughter's of a pretty age.
Nurse	Faith, I can tell her age unto an hour.
Lady Capulet	She's not fourteen.
Nurse	I'll lay fourteen of my teeth (and yet, to my teen be it spoken, I have but four), she's not fourteen. How long 15 is it now to Lammas-tide?
Lady Capulet	A fortnight and odd days.
Nurse	Even or odd, of all days in the year, come Lammas- eve at night shall she be fourteen. Susan and she (God rest all Christian souls) were of an age. Well, Susan 20 is with God, she was too good for me. But, as I said, on Lammas Eve at night shall she be fourteen, that shall she. Marry; I remember it well. 'Tis since the earthquake now eleven years, and she was weaned (I never shall forget it) of all the days of the year, upon 25 that day, for I had then laid wormwood to my dug, sitting in the sun under the dove-house wall. My lord and you were then at Mantua (nay I do bear a brain). But, as I said, when it did taste the wormwood on the

87–8 When the devout religion ... such falsehood: when my loving eye tells me such a lie

90–1 these who often drowned ... Transparent heretics: these eyes that wept for love so often couldn't betray that love

94 none else being by: with no other beauties nearby

95 poised with: balanced against

96 that crystal scales: your eyes

97 Your lady's love: the love you have for Rosaline

99 she shall scant show well that now seems best: and the one you love best now will not seem anywhere near as beautiful

101 splendour of mine own: in how much more beautiful my love is than the rest

Director's Note, 1.2

- ✔ Paris asks permission to marry Juliet. Capulet asks him to wait, because she is too young, but gives him hope and invites him to the feast.
- ✔ Romeo and Benvolio find out the girl Romeo loves, Rosaline, is invited to the feast.
- ✔ Benvolio says they should go to the feast, to see that there are many more attractive women than Rosaline.
- ✔ How does Shakespeare mix humour and keep the story moving?

2 maidenhead: virginity

3 bade: told her to

7 What is your will?: what can I do for you?

8 the matter: what I want to discuss

8 give leave: leave us

10 thou's hear our counsel: you shall hear our discussion

11 pretty age: suitable age for marriage

14 teen: sorrow

15 but: only

16 Lammas-tide: a holy day, 1 August

19 Susan: the Nurse's daughter

20 of an age: the same age

24 was weaned: stopped breast-feeding

26 laid wormwood to my dug: put a bitter liquid on her nipple (to put the baby off breast-feeding)

28 nay I do bear a brain: haven't I got a good memory

A

B

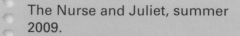

The Nurse and Juliet, summer 2009.

One of these photos was taken at line 31, and the other at line 56. Which do you think is which? Quote from the text to support your answer.

Penny Layden, Ellie Kendrick

SHAKESPEARE'S WORLD

Juliet's relationship with her mother and her Nurse

There were many different types of servants in Elizabethan households, both men and women. They had different status depending on their exact duties. Some worked for a family for many years (often all their lives). Others had a contract to work for a set period of time. Many of these servants were teenagers. Servants were given food and board in exchange for their work. Most were also paid a wage.

Although the Nurse is a servant, Shakespeare shows her as closer to Juliet than her mother is. This would not be unusual at the time. The Nurse's speech tells us she has been with the family at least since Juliet's birth. She helped raise Juliet from infancy. Aside from breast-feeding Juliet as a baby, the Nurse would have looked after Juliet's clothes and helped Juliet dress. She would have slept in Juliet's room at night. She also gave Juliet advice, and was her only trusted friend. Juliet spent more time with her than with the rest of her family. This level of friendship is not unusual amongst masters and servants in Shakespeare's plays. Desdemona and Emilia in *Othello* and Portia and Nerissa in *The Merchant of Venice* are close as well. Regardless of these friendships, however, servants were expected to respect and obey their masters. There was a hierarchy among servants too. Less important servants were expected to respect and obey more important ones. We see this in the play. Peter carries the Nurse's fan, although they are both servants.

SHAKESPEARE'S WORLD

Arranged marriage and age at marriage

In Shakespeare's time, women typically married at age 24 to 26. Men usually waited until age 27 to 29. Many men had to finish an apprenticeship and save money to set up a home. People were encouraged to marry someone of a similar age and social class, so children of wealthy, important people had fewer suitable choices. Children of well-off families also married younger – because they didn't have to save enough money to set up a home. Their parents often arranged marriages for them, just as Capulet does.

A woman from a middle- or upper-class family had less choice over who she married than a man did. Her father negotiated a marriage contract for her. This said how much he would give as a dowry (money or property given to her husband on the wedding day), and who would support her if her husband died.

nipple of my dug and felt it bitter, pretty fool, to see it   30
tetchy and fall out with the dug. Shake quoth the dove-
house: 'twas no need, I trow, to bid me trudge. And
since that time it is eleven years, for then she could
stand alone. Nay, by th' rood, she could have run and
waddled all about. For even the day before, she broke   35
her brow: and then my husband (God be with his soul,
a' was a merry man) took up the child, "Yea", quoth he,
"dost thou fall upon thy face? Thou wilt fall backward
when thou hast more wit, Wilt thou not, Jule?" And, by
my holidam, the pretty wretch left crying and said "Ay".   40
To see now how a jest shall come about. I warrant, and
I should live a thousand years, I never should forget
it. "Wilt thou not, Jule?" quoth he, and, pretty fool it
stinted and said "Ay".

Lady Capulet   Enough of this, I pray thee, hold thy peace.   45

Nurse   Yes, madam, yet I cannot choose but laugh,
To think it should leave crying and say "Ay".
And yet, I warrant, it had upon its brow
A bump as big as a young cockerel's stone.
A perilous knock, and it cried bitterly.   50
"Yea", quoth my husband, "fall'st upon thy face?
Thou wilt fall backward when thou comest to age,
Wilt thou not, Jule?" It stinted and said "Ay".

Juliet   And stint thou too, I pray thee nurse, say I.

Nurse   Peace, I have done, God mark thee to his grace,   55
Thou wast the prettiest babe that e'er I nursed.
And I might live to see thee married once,
I have my wish.

Lady Capulet   Marry, that "marry" is the very theme
I came to talk of. Tell me, daughter Juliet,   60
How stands your disposition to be married?

Juliet   It is an honour that I dream not of.

Nurse   An honour! Were not I thine only nurse,
I would say thou hadst sucked wisdom from thy teat.

Lady Capulet   Well, think of marriage now. Younger than you   65
Here in Verona, ladies of esteem,
Are made already mothers. By my count
I was your mother much upon these years
That you are now a maid. Thus then in brief:
The valiant Paris seeks you for his love.   70

Nurse   A man, young lady. Lady, such a man
As all the world. Why, he's a man of wax.

Lady Capulet   Verona's summer hath not such a flower.

Nurse   Nay he's a flower, in faith a very flower.

Lady Capulet   What say you, can you love the gentleman?   75
This night you shall behold him at our feast.
Read o'er the volume of young Paris' face,

---

29 **it:** the baby, Juliet

31 **tetchy and fall out with the dug:** cross and dislike feeding

31–2 **Shake quoth the dove-house:** the dove-house shook in the earthquake

32 **'twas no need, I trow, to bid me trudge:** in truth, it didn't need to do that just to make me move

34 **by th' rood:** by Christ's cross (a way of swearing you are telling the truth)

35–6 **broke her brow:** cut her forehead

37 **a':** he

38 **Thou wilt fall backward:** sexual double meaning

39 **thou hast more wit:** you're wiser

39–40 **by my holidam:** by my holy lady (a way of swearing you are telling the truth)

40 **left:** stopped

41 **come about:** come true

41 **warrant:** swear it's true

44 **stinted:** stopped (crying)

45 **hold thy peace:** that's enough talking

47 **it:** the baby, Juliet

49 **stone:** testicle

52 **comest to age:** are old enough

57 **And I might:** if I could just

57 **once:** one day

59 **Marry:** a mild oath – by Mary (Christ's mother)

61 **How stands your disposition:** how do you feel about ...

64 **thy teat:** the breast that fed you

66 **ladies of esteem:** well-respected women of good social status

68–9 **much upon these years ... now a maid:** at about your age

72 **a man of wax:** as perfect as a wax model of the perfect man

76 **behold:** see

77 **Read o'er the volume of young Paris' face:** Lady Capulet uses a book metaphor throughout this speech; Juliet has to 'read' Paris' potential as a husband

Text focus: Act 1 Scene 3 lines 54–95

Your GCSE Literature exam will focus on one extract question and one essay question. The extract question will be assessed through the objectives (in bold) below.

(AO1) Response to characters and events:
- The Nurse is both Juliet's close companion and a trusted family servant of Lady Capulet. *Find evidence of these roles.*
- Juliet is closer to her nurse than to her mother. The Nurse's bawdy banter, which embarrasses Juliet, is a reminder of the physical side of love.
- Lady Capulet speaks of society and of Paris's appearance, not of emotion. *What do you think are Lady Capulet's motives in marrying Juliet to Paris?*

(AO2) Language, structure and form:
- Lady Capulet's language is neutral and abstract – "How stands your disposition" – and is unlike any traditional language of love.
- Juliet's formal language with her mother is a contrast to the way she speaks to the nurse. *What does this show about Juliet's relationship with these two women?*
- The Nurse's image of Paris as a man of wax has a double meaning: a model man but also a malleable (easily influenced) one. *Decide which aspect of his character would most appeal to Juliet's mother and which to the Nurse.*
- Shakespeare uses the plan to marry Juliet to Paris to drive the plot forward.

Question:
How is the relationship between Juliet, her mother and the Nurse presented in this extract? (15 marks)

Director's Note, 1.3

✔ Lady Capulet tells Juliet about Paris' wish to marry her.
✔ Juliet is dutiful, and says she will look to like Paris, but only so far as her mother approves.
✔ This is the first time we see Juliet. What picture of her does Shakespeare present?

SHAKESPEARE'S WORLD
◇◇◇◇◇◇◇◇◇◇◇◇◇◇

Boys and men playing women

During Shakespeare's lifetime, women were not allowed to act in public theatres. The leading female roles, like Juliet, were played by teenage boys before their voices broke. The acting companies only had a few such boys. Some female characters were played by men. They were usually the older, comic female parts, such as the Nurse (seen here played by a man, Bette Bourne). This gave Shakespeare the chance to write for the humorous possibility of a man dressed as a woman, which is a popular form of comedy to this day.

And find delight writ there with beauty's pen.
Examine every married lineament,
And see how one another lends content. 80
And what obscured in this fair volume lies,
Find written in the margent of his eyes.
This precious book of love, this unbound lover,
To beautify him, only lacks a cover.
The fish lives in the sea, and 'tis much pride, 85
For fair without, the fair within to hide.
That book in many's eyes doth share the glory,
That in gold clasps, locks in the golden story.
So shall you share all that he doth possess,
By having him, making yourself no less. 90

Nurse No less? Nay, bigger! Women grow by men.

Lady Capulet Speak briefly, can you like of Paris' love?

Juliet I'll look to like, if looking liking move.
But no more deep will I endart mine eye
Than your consent gives strength to make it fly. 95

Enter Servant.

Peter Madam, the guests are come, supper served up, you
called, my young lady asked for, the nurse cursed in
the pantry, and everything in extremity. I must hence to
wait. I beseech you follow straight. *Exit Peter.*

Lady Capulet We follow thee. Juliet, the County stays. 100

Nurse Go, girl, seek happy nights to happy days. *Exit all.*

ACT 1 SCENE 4

*Enter torch-bearers, Romeo, Mercutio, Benvolio, with five
or six friends as masquers.*

Romeo What, shall this speech be spoke for our excuse?
Or shall we on without apology?

Benvolio The date is out of such prolixity.
We'll have no Cupid hoodwinked with a scarf,
Bearing a Tartar's painted bow of lath, 5
Scaring the ladies like a crow-keeper;
Nor no without-book prologue, faintly spoke
After the prompter, for our entrance.
But let them measure us by what they will,
We'll measure them a measure, and be gone. 10

Romeo Give me a torch, I am not for this ambling.
Being but heavy I will bear the light.

Mercutio Nay, gentle Romeo, we must have you dance.

Romeo Not I, believe me. You have dancing shoes
With nimble soles, I have a soul of lead 15
So stakes me to the ground I cannot move.

Mercutio You are a lover; borrow Cupid's wings
And soar with them above a common bound.

---

79 married lineament: feature of his face
81 what obscured in this fair volume lies: what you can't tell from that
82 margent: margin (some people write comments in book margins)
83 unbound: double meaning: incomplete because unmarried; a book with no cover
86 For fair without, the fair within to hide: Juliet will complete him, she the beautiful cover, he the book inside
90 no less: as important as he is
91 grow: double meaning: grow in status; become pregnant
92 like of: accept
93 I'll look to like, if looking liking move: I'll go hoping to like him
94–5 no more deep will I endart ... to make it fly: I won't like him any more than you think I should
98 in extremity: needs doing at once
98–9 to wait: to serve the food and drink
99 straight: straight away
100 the County stays: the Count is waiting

SD masquers: masked entertainers

1 this speech be spoke for our excuse: we have a speech ready (masquers often gave a speech on arrival)
3 The date is out of such prolixity: it isn't fashionable to make speeches any more
4 hoodwinked: blindfolded
5 Tartar's painted bow of lath: a bow made from cheap wood, like a stage prop
6 crow-keeper: scarecrow
7 Nor no without-book prologue: nor any speech learned by heart
9 measure us: judge us
10 measure them a measure: give them a dance
11 I am not for this ambling: I don't want to dance

16 So stakes me: fixes me

18 common bound: normal limit

23

Romeo	I am too sore enpiercèd with his shaft
	To soar with his light feathers, and so bound
	I cannot bound a pitch above dull woe.
	Under love's heavy burden do I sink.
Mercutio	And, to sink in it, should you burden love, Romeo
	Too great oppression for a tender thing.
Romeo	Is love a tender thing? It is too rough,
	Too rude, too boisterous, and it pricks like thorn.
Mercutio	If love be rough with you, be rough with love,
	Prick love for pricking, and you beat love down.
	Give me a case to put my visage in,
	A visor for a visor. What care I
	What curious eye doth quote deformities?
	Here are the beetle brows shall blush for me.
Benvolio	Come, knock and enter; and no sooner in,
	But every man betake him to his legs.
Romeo	A torch for me. Let wantons light of heart
	Tickle the senseless rushes with their heels,
	For I am proverbed with a grandsire phrase;
	I'll be a candle-holder and look on,
	The game was ne'er so fair, and I am done.
Mercutio	Tut, dun's the mouse, the constable's own word.
	If thou art dun, we'll draw thee from the mire
	Or, (save your reverence) love, wherein thou stickest
	Up to the ears. Come, we burn daylight, ho!
Romeo	Nay, that's not so.
Mercutio	I mean, sir, in delay
	We waste our lights in vain, like lamps by day.
	Take our good meaning, for our judgement sits
	Five times in that, ere once in our five wits.
Romeo	And we mean well in going to this masque,
	But 'tis no wit to go.
Mercutio	Why, may one ask?
Romeo	I dreamt a dream to-night.
Mercutio	And so did I.
Romeo	Well, what was yours?
Mercutio	That dreamers often lie.
Romeo	In bed asleep, while they do dream things true.
Mercutio	O, then, I see Queen Mab hath been with you.
Benvolio	Queen Mab, what's she?
Mercutio	She is the fairies' midwife, and she comes
	In shape no bigger than an agate-stone
	On the fore-finger of an alderman,
	Drawn with a team of little atomies

19 sore enpiercèd with his shaft: deeply in love, pierced by Cupid's arrow

20 and so bound: and held back like this

23-4 to sink in it ... for a tender thing: be careful not to put too great a burden on something as easily damaged as love

28 Prick love for pricking, and you beat love down: act on your feelings and you will control love, not be controlled by it

29 a case to put my visage in: a mask to wear

30 A visor for a visor: a mask to hide my face

31 What curious eye doth quote deformities: if people gossip about how ugly I am

32 beetle brows: thick eyebrows (the mask)

34 betake him to his legs: start dancing

35 wantons: pleasure-seekers

36 Tickle the senseless rushes with their heels: dance

37 proverbed with a grandsire phrase: in the words of the proverb

39 The game was ne'er so fair: and see more of what's going on

40 dun's the mouse: be quiet and don't draw attention

40 the constable's own word: as a night watchman might say

41 draw thee from the mire: pull you out of the mud

42 save your reverence: excuse my rudeness

43 burn daylight: waste time

46 good meaning: the sense of what I say

46-7 for our judgement sits ... five wits: because that's five times better than what our senses tell us

49 'tis no wit to go: it isn't wise to go

52 while: sometimes

53 Queen Mab: a powerful fairy

55 fairies' midwife: the fairy who delivers dreams to humans

56 agate-stone: agate was used to make rings carved with tiny pictures

57 alderman: an important town councillor

Over men's noses as they lie asleep.
Her chariot is an empty hazel-nut   60
Made by the joiner squirrel or old grub,
Time out o' mind the fairies' coachmakers.
Her wagon-spokes made of long spinners' legs,
The cover of the wings of grasshoppers,
The traces of the smallest spider's web,   65
The collars of the moonshine's watery beams,
Her whip of cricket's bone, the lash of film,
Her wagoner a small grey-coated gnat,
Not so big as a round little worm
Pricked from the lazy finger of a maid;   70
And in this state she gallops night by night:
Through lovers' brains, and then they dream of love;
O'er courtiers' knees, that dream on curtsies straight;
O'er lawyers' fingers, who straight dream on fees;
O'er ladies' lips, who straight on kisses dream;   75
Which oft the angry Mab with blisters plagues,
Because their breaths with sweetmeats tainted are.
Sometime she gallops o'er a courtier's nose,
And then dreams he of smelling out a suit;
And sometime comes she with a tithe-pig's tail,   80
Tickling a parson's nose as 'a lies asleep,
Then he dreams of another benefice.
Sometime she driveth o'er a soldier's neck,
And then dreams he of cutting foreign throats,
Of breaches, ambuscadoes, Spanish blades,   85
Of healths five-fathom deep, and then anon
Drums in his ear, at which he starts and wakes,
And being thus frighted, swears a prayer or two
And sleeps again. This is that very Mab
That plaits the manes of horses in the night,   90
And bakes the elflocks in foul sluttish hairs,
Which once untangled, much misfortune bodes.
This is the hag, when maids lie on their backs,
That presses them and learns them first to bear,
Making them women of good carriage.   95
This is she—

Romeo   Peace, peace, Mercutio, peace,
Thou talk'st of nothing.

---

58 **atomies:** tiny creatures
61 **joiner:** carpenter
62 **Time out o' mind:** for as long as anyone can remember
63 **spinners:** spiders
65 **traces:** harness
66 **collars:** neck straps joined to the harness
67 **film:** very, very thin threads
68 **wagoner:** driver
71 **state:** magnificence
73 **courtiers:** socially important people who are part of a royal court
73 **curtsies:** bowing to the king or queen
76 **oft:** often
77 **sweetmeats:** sweet food
77 **tainted:** spoiled
79 **smelling out a suit:** finding someone who will reward him for taking their request to the king or queen
80 **tithe-pig:** people had to give a tenth of their income to the Church (tithe); poorer people paid in crops or animals
82 **benefice:** paid work for the Church
85 **breaches, ambuscadoes, Spanish blades:** breaking down castle walls, ambushes, the best Spanish swords
86 **healths five-fathom deep:** drinking toasts with a lot of wine
91 **bakes the elflocks in foul sluttish hairs:** tangles unbrushed hair
92 **much misfortune bodes:** means bad luck
94 **bear:** carry the weight of a man during sex or a baby in pregnancy. This is the start of a series of sexual double meanings
95 **of good carriage:** able to bear these weights
97 **nothing:** a double meaning: 1) nothing; 2) a slang reference to the vagina at the time, 'no-thing'

---

exam SKILLS

Target skill: analysing language

Question: How does Shakespeare present Mercutio's character through his language?

Shakespeare uses this speech to show Mercutio is a witty and imaginative man. His speech is similarly dynamic, and full of puns and lively images.

1 Read Mercutio's account of Queen Mab in lines 55–72.

What do you notice about:
• the choice of words; • the creatures mentioned;
• the use of repetition; • the pace of the lines; • the images;
• the change of mood in the speech?

2 What might an audience learn about Mercutio's character when he admits his talk was "begot of nothing but vain fantasy"?

Mercutio	True, I talk of dreams,
	Which are the children of an idle brain,
	Begot of nothing but vain fantasy,
	Which is as thin of substance as the air
	And more inconstant than the wind, who woos
	Even now the frozen bosom of the north.
	And being angered, puffs away from thence,
	Turning his side to the dew-dropping south.
Benvolio	This wind, you talk of blows us from ourselves,
	Supper is done, and we shall come too late.
Romeo	I fear, too early, for my mind misgives,
	Some consequence yet hanging in the stars
	Shall bitterly begin his fearful date
	With this night's revels, and expire the term
	Of a despisèd life closed in my breast
	By some vile forfeit of untimely death.
	But he that hath the steerage of my course,
	Direct my sail. On, lusty gentlemen.
Benvolio	Strike drum.

100

105

110

115

99 **Begot:** born of

104 **Turning his side:** changing direction

105 **blows us from ourselves:** distracts us

107 **my mind misgives:** I have a bad feeling about this

108 **yet hanging in the stars:** fated to happen in the future

109–10 **Shall bitterly begin … this night's revels:** will be set in motion at this party

110–2 **and expire the term … untimely death:** ending with my death

113 **he that hath the steerage of my course:** God, who guides my life

They march about the stage, and stand to one side.

exam SKILLS

Target skill: commenting on themes

Question: How does Shakespeare present the theme of fate in lines 107–114?

A theme is an important idea that features throughout a text. Recurring references enable us to see different aspects of an idea and understand a play's messages.

Fate is one of the themes in *The Tragedy of Romeo and Juliet*. Shakespeare signalled in the Prologue that Romeo and Juliet are "star-crossed lovers". In lines 107–114 there is a sense of impending doom, even before Romeo has met Juliet.

Working with a partner, rank the statements below in order of your agreement with them.

a) Romeo's earlier moodiness has become a feeling that his "despisèd life" is doomed to end with "untimely death".

b) Romeo is not portrayed convincingly here – he is just a mouthpiece for the theme of fate.

c) Romeo thinks his future has been decided for him.

d) There is an element of free will in Romeo's actions.

e) His speech puts the audience in an omnipotent position, looking over events.

Director's Note, 1.4

✔ Romeo, Benvolio, Mercutio and friends are on the way to Capulet's feast, disguised by their masks.

✔ Romeo is worried by a dream.

✔ Mercutio mocks him, telling him about Queen Mab.

✔ What does Shakespeare tell us in this scene about the characters of Romeo and Mercutio?

SHAKESPEARE'S WORLD

Masques and masks

In the Tudor and Stuart periods, the upper classes held grand celebrations in their own houses. The family hired musicians and actors. They also took an active part themselves, often in masques. Masques could be anything from a simple fancy-dress party (where everyone wore a mask) to a full-scale theatrical show, with long speeches and elaborate special effects. Henry VIII was very fond of masques, and regularly acted in them. James I took a less active part, but enjoyed masques in his court. Shakespeare wrote both types of masque in his plays. The one in *The Tempest* is especially elaborate. In *Romeo and Juliet* only the younger characters wear masks and dance. This, then, is a simple masque. It is a chance for the youth of Verona to flirt with each other, whilst under the cover of disguise. Crucially, it gives Romeo and his friends the chance to enter the Capulet household without being detected.

ACT 1 SCENE 5

Enter servingmen, including Peter, with dishclothes.

Peter	Where's Potpan, that he helps not to take away? He shift a trencher? He scrape a trencher!
First Servant	When good manners shall lie all in one or two men's hands and they unwashed too, 'tis a foul thing.
Peter	Away with the joint-stools, remove the court-cupboard, 5 look to the plate. Good thou, save me a piece of marchpane, and, as thou lovest me, let the porter let in Susan Grindstone and Nell. — Anthony and Potpan!
Second Servant	Ay, boy, ready.
Peter	You are looked for and called for, asked for and sought 10 for, in the great chamber.
First Servant	We cannot be here and there too. Cheerly boys, be brisk awhile, and the longer liver take all.

Exit Peter and the servants.

*Enter Capulet, Capulet's cousin, Lady Capulet, Juliet,
Tybalt, all the guests and gentlewomen. Romeo and the
masquers join them.*

Capulet	Welcome, gentlemen. Ladies that have their toes Unplagued with corns will walk about with you. 15 Ah, my mistresses, which of you all Will now deny to dance? She that makes dainty, She, I'll swear, hath corns. Am I come near ye now? Welcome, gentlemen! I have seen the day That I have worn a visor and could tell 20 A whispering tale in a fair lady's ear, Such as would please. 'Tis gone, 'tis gone, 'tis gone. You are welcome, gentlemen! Come, musicians, play.

Music plays and they dance.

	A hall, a hall, give room, and foot it, girls. More light, you knaves, and turn the tables up, 25 And quench the fire, the room is grown too hot. Ah, sirrah, this unlooked-for sport comes well. Nay, sit, nay, sit, good cousin Capulet, For you and I are past our dancing days. How long is't now since last yourself and I 30 Were in a masque?
Capulet's Cousin	By'r lady, thirty years.
Capulet	What, man! 'Tis not so much, 'tis not so much: 'Tis since the nuptial of Lucentio, Come Pentecost as quickly as it will, Some five and twenty years, and then we masked. 35
Capulet Cousin	'Tis more, 'tis more, his son is elder, sir. His son is thirty.

Glossary

1 **take away:** clear the table
2 **trencher:** wooden plate

4 **foul:** dirty

5 **joint-stools:** stools
5 **court-cupboard:** sideboard
6 **look to the plate:** make sure no one steals the silver
6 **Good thou:** Do me a favour, will you
7 **marchpane:** marzipan

11 **great chamber:** main hall

13 **the longer liver take all:** whoever survives gets it all

15 **walk about:** dance

17 **deny to:** refuse to
17 **makes dainty:** holds back
18 **Am I come near ye now?:** have I hit on the truth?

24 **A hall:** (to the servants) make room (for the dancing)
24 **foot it:** dance
25 **turn the tables up:** put the tables away

27 **unlooked-for sport:** surprise entertainment (the masquers)

31 **By'r lady:** by our lady (Christ's mother)
33 **nuptial:** wedding
34 **Come Pentecost as quickly as it will:** years pass so quickly

ACT 1 SCENE 5

Capulet
                           Will you tell me that?
His son was but a ward two years ago.

Romeo
[To a Servingman.]
What lady is that which doth enrich the hand
Of yonder knight?

Servingman
I know not, sir.

Romeo
O, she doth teach the torches to burn bright!
It seems she hangs upon the cheek of night
As a rich jewel in an Ethiope's ear.
Beauty too rich for use, for earth too dear.
So shows a snowy dove trooping with crows,
As yonder lady o'er her fellows shows.
The measure done, I'll watch her place of stand,
And touching hers, make blessèd my rude hand.
Did my heart love till now? Forswear it sight,
For I ne'er saw true beauty till this night.

38 **a ward:** someone not old enough to run their own affairs, so has a guardian

40

44 **Ethiope:** a black African (from Ethiopia)
45 **Beauty too rich ... too dear:** too beautiful to live an ordinary life on earth
48 **The measure done:** now this dance is over
49 **rude:** rough, unworthy
50 **Forswear it sight:** deny it, my eyes

45

50

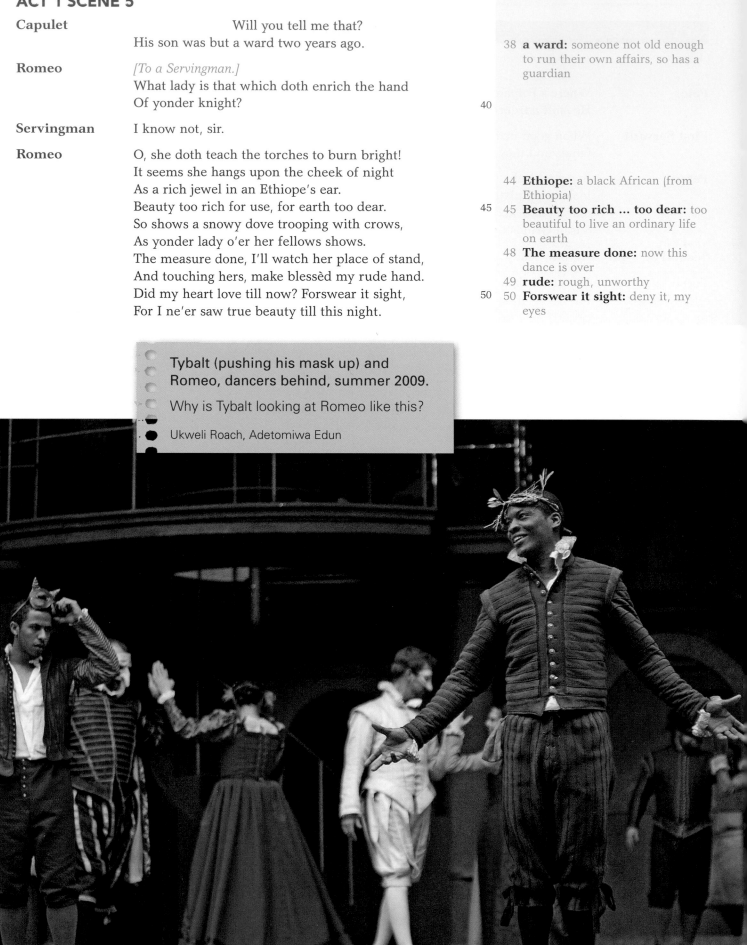

Tybalt (pushing his mask up) and Romeo, dancers behind, summer 2009.

Why is Tybalt looking at Romeo like this?

Ukweli Roach, Adetomiwa Edun

Tybalt	This, by his voice, should be a Montague.
	Fetch me my rapier, boy. *[Exit Page.]*
	What, dares the slave
	Come hither covered with an antic face,
	To fleer and scorn at our solemnity? 55
	Now, by the stock and honour of my kin,
	To strike him dead I hold it not a sin.
Capulet	Why, how now, kinsman, wherefore storm you so?
Tybalt	Uncle, this is a Montague, our foe
	A villain that is hither come in spite, 60
	To scorn at our solemnity this night.
Capulet	Young Romeo is it?
Tybalt	'Tis he, that villain Romeo.
Capulet	Content thee, gentle coz, let him alone,
	'A bears him like a portly gentleman, 65
	And to say truth, Verona brags of him
	To be a virtuous and well-governed youth.
	I would not for the wealth of all the town
	Here in my house do him disparagement,
	Therefore be patient, take no note of him. 70
	It is my will, the which if thou respect,
	Show a fair presence and put off these frowns,
	An ill-beseeming semblance for a feast.
Tybalt	It fits, when such a villain is a guest.
	I'll not endure him.
Capulet	He shall be endured. 75
	What, goodman boy! I say he shall! Go to!
	Am I the master here or you? Go to!
	You'll not endure him? God shall mend my soul!
	You'll make a mutiny among my guests!
	You will set cock-a-hoop! You'll be the man! 80
Tybalt	Why, uncle, 'tis a shame.
Capulet	Go to, go to!
	You are a saucy boy. Is't so indeed?
	This trick may chance to scathe you. I know what,
	You must contrary me! Marry, 'tis time. —
	Well said, my hearts. — You are a princox, go, 85
	Be quiet, or — More light, more light for shame —
	I'll make you quiet. — What, cheerly my hearts!
Tybalt	Patience perforce with wilful choler meeting,
	Makes my flesh tremble in their different greeting.
	I will withdraw, but this intrusion shall 90
	Now seeming sweet, convert to bitter gall. *Exit.*
Romeo	*[To Juliet.]* If I profane with my unworthiest hand
	This holy shrine, the gentle sin is this,
	My lips, two blushing pilgrims, ready stand
	To smooth that rough touch with a tender kiss. 95
Juliet	Good pilgrim, you do wrong your hand too much,
	Which mannerly devotion shows in this,

53 **rapier:** sword
53 **slave:** used as an insult
54 **hither:** here
54 **antic face:** mask
55 **fleer and scorn at our solemnity:** mock our celebration
56 **the stock and honour of my kin:** my family's honour
58 **wherefore storm you so?:** why are you so angry?
60 **in spite:** showing us no respect

64 **Content thee:** don't be so angry
65 **'A bears him like a portly gentleman:** he's behaving perfectly well
67 **well-governed:** well-behaved
69 **do him disparagement:** insult him
70 **note:** notice
72 **Show a fair presence:** be cheerful
73 **An ill-beseeming semblance:** which are not appropriate

76 **goodman boy:** an insult suggesting Tybalt isn't behaving like a gentleman
76 **Go to!:** that's enough of this
79 **make a mutiny:** disobey me
80 **set cock-a-hoop:** go wild
80 **be the man:** take the decisions
81 **'tis a shame:** it brings shame on us
82 **saucy:** disgracefully rude
83 **trick may chance to scathe you:** behaving like this won't do you any good
84 **contrary:** oppose
84 **Marry, 'tis time ... :** a mild oath – by Mary (Christ's mother). For the next few lines, Capulet is talking to his guests, his servants and Tybalt in quick succession
88–9 **Patience perforce ... different greeting:** this clash between enforced patience and my anger makes me shake

92 **profane:** mistreat a holy object
93 **This holy shrine:** Juliet's hand
94 **pilgrims:** travellers to holy places
96 **you do wrong:** you are unkind to
97 **mannerly devotion shows in this:** is acting with proper respect

29

PALM TO PALM

In Act 1 Scene 5 Romeo and Juliet meet for the first time (lines 92–109).

- In pairs, one person read Romeo, and one read Juliet.
- After your first read-through, identify the last word of each line, and whether it is part of a rhyme.
- Now stand opposite each other to read the text aloud.
- Every time your line rhymes with another of your lines, take **one step** forward.
- Romeo, every time your line rhymes with Juliet's line, take **two steps** forward.
- Juliet, every time your line rhymes with Romeo's line, take **two steps** forward.

1 Which character makes the first move?

2 Is there a pattern in the movement?

3 What does this scene reveal about
   a) Juliet's personality?
   b) Romeo's personality?

4 What metaphors do the characters use to express their feelings and intentions?

Romeo and Juliet, spring 2009.

Pick a line from the text on the opposite page which could be used as a caption for this photo. Give reasons for your choice.

James Alexandrou, Lorraine Burroughs

Director's view

Dominic Dromgoole
Director, summer 2009

It is the essence of a lot of Shakespeare's writing – his ability to paint a broad social landscape as a backdrop, and then pick out moments of human drama and juggle three or four different stories very deftly and very quickly at the same time.

Everyone is looking forward to Romeo and Juliet getting together. Everyone is hungry for the moment when they lock eyes on each other, and you can play on that. Tybalt is a wonderful spoiler, and he is a great energy – just as a sort of malevolent energy. Capulet, we have already got to know, we know that he is anxious, a slightly overzealous, over keen host. We work out very quickly there is some sort of dysfunction between him and his wife. So it is full of stories that have already been quite deftly built up, and they reach a very quick climax in that scene.

For saints have hands, that pilgrims' hands do touch,
And palm to palm is holy palmers' kiss.

Romeo Have not saints lips, and holy palmers too? 100

Juliet Ay, pilgrim, lips that they must use in prayer.

Romeo O, then, dear saint, let lips do what hands do;
They pray (grant thou) lest faith turn to despair.

Juliet Saints do not move, though grant for prayers' sake.

Romeo Then move not, while my prayer's effect I take. 105

[They kiss.]

Thus from my lips, by thine, my sin is purged.

Juliet Then have my lips the sin that they have took.

Romeo Sin from my lips? O trespass sweetly urged!
Give me my sin again.   *[They kiss.]*

Juliet   You kiss by th' book.

Nurse Madam, your mother craves a word with you. 110

[Juliet moves away.]

Romeo What is her mother?

Nurse   Marry, bachelor,
Her mother is the lady of the house,
And a good lady, and a wise and virtuous
I nursed her daughter, that you talked withal.
I tell you, he that can lay hold of her 115
Shall have the chinks.

Romeo *[Aside.]*   Is she a Capulet?
O dear account! My life is my foe's debt.

Benvolio Away, begone, the sport is at the best.

Romeo Ay, so I fear; the more is my unrest.

Capulet Nay, gentlemen, prepare not to be gone, 120
We have a trifling foolish banquet towards.
Is it e'en so? Why then I thank you all.
I thank you, honest gentlemen, good night.
More torches here! — Come on then, let's to bed.
Ah, sirrah, by my faith, it waxes late: 125
I'll to my rest.

[They all exit, except Juliet and the Nurse.]

Juliet Come hither, nurse. What is yond gentleman?

Nurse The son and heir of old Tiberio.

Juliet What's he that now is going out of door?

Nurse Marry, that I think be young Petruchio. 130

Juliet What's he that follows here, that would not dance?

Nurse I know not.

---

99 **palmers:** name for pilgrims to the Holy Land, who came back with a palm leaf

99 **palm to palm is holy palmers' kiss:** it's more appropriate for palmers to touch hands in greeting, not kiss

104 **grant for prayers' sake:** they answer prayers

105 **my prayer's effect:** a kiss

106 **purged:** cleaned away

108 **urged:** argued for

109 **You kiss by th' book:** in just the right way

111 **What:** who

114 **withal:** with

115 **lay hold of:** marry

116 **the chinks:** the money
117 **dear account:** what a high price
117 **My life is my foe's debt:** an enemy holds my life in her hands
118 **the sport is at the best:** we've had the best of it
119 **the more is my unrest:** that's what bothers me
121 **We have a ... towards:** we're just going to have a bite to eat
122 **Is it e'en so?:** must you really go?

125 **it waxes:** it is getting

127 **yond:** over there

31

THE MASKED BALL

Act 1 Scene 5 is Capulet's feast. Shakespeare created a scene with lots of people, where the audience focuses on just a couple of people at any one time.

Read the Shakespeare's World box on page 26.

- In groups, read through the Working Cut, noting the stage directions. Which words in the characters' lines suggest a change of focus? How could you tell?

- Now break down the Working Cut into sections. Give each section a name.

- Make a table with three columns: *Section name*, *Characters* and *Function in the scene*. Complete the table with the answers you have worked out.

SECTION NAME	CHARACTERS	FUNCTION IN THE SCENE
Setting the scene	The servants	Creates the feeling of bustle: the feast is important
Welcome	Capulets and masquers	Shows Capulet as friendly host

1 The tone of the exchange between Capulet and Tybalt (lines 52–91) is very different from the tone of the conversation between Romeo and Juliet (lines 92–110). *How does Shakespeare do this?*

2 Romeo and Juliet's words are full of religious imagery. *Which image do you think is the most memorable?*

3 Their love is poetic – Romeo speaks in rhyming couplets (lines 42–51) and in lines 92–110 the two young lovers break into a sonnet (a 14-line poem which rhymes *abab cdcd efef gg*). *Which lines make the sonnet?*

Working Cut – text for experiment

Enter Servingmen, including Peter, with dishclothes.

Pet   Away with the joint-stools,— Anthony and Potpan!

2nd S.   Ay, boy, ready.

Pet   You are looked for and called for, asked for and sought for, in the great chamber.

1st S.   We cannot be here and there too.

Exit Peter and the servants.

Enter Capulet, Capulet's cousin, Lady Capulet, Juliet, Tybalt, all the guests and gentlewomen. Romeo and the masquers join them.

Cap   Welcome, gentlemen. Ladies that have their toes
Unplagued with corns will walk about with you.

Music plays and they dance.

Rom   *[To a Servingman.]* What lady is that?

Serv.   I know not, sir.

Rom   O, she doth teach the torches to burn bright!

Tyb   This, by his voice, should be a Montague.
Fetch me my rapier, boy. *[Exit Page.]*
Uncle, this is a Montague, our foe

Cap   Young Romeo is it?
Content thee, gentle coz, let him alone

Tyb   I'll not endure him.

Cap   Go to, go to!

Tyb   I will withdraw, but this intrusion shall
Now seeming sweet, convert to bitter gall. *Exit.*

Rom   *[To Juliet.]* If I profane with my unworthiest hand
This holy shrine, the gentle sin is this,
My lips, two blushing pilgrims, ready stand
To smooth that rough touch with a tender kiss.

Jul   Good pilgrim, you do wrong your hand too much,
Which mannerly devotion shows in this,
For saints have hands, that pilgrims' hands do touch,
And palm to palm is holy palmers' kiss.

Rom   Have not saints lips, and holy palmers too?

Jul   Ay, pilgrim, lips that they must use in prayer.

Rom   O, then, dear saint, let lips do what hands do;
They pray (grant thou) lest faith turn to despair.

Jul   Saints do not move, though grant for prayers' sake.
[They kiss.]

Nurse   Madam, your mother craves a word with you.
[Juliet moves away.]

Romeo   What is her mother?

Nurse   Her mother is the lady of the house.

Ben   Away, begone, the sport is at the best.
[They all exit, except Juliet and the Nurse.]

Juliet   Come hither, nurse. What is yond gentleman?

Nurse   I know not.

Juliet   Go ask his name. *[She goes.]*

Nurse   His name is Romeo, and a Montague;

Juliet   My only love sprung from my only hate!
[Someone calls within, 'Juliet!'.]

Nurse   Come let's away, the strangers all are gone.

Juliet	Go ask his name.	*[She goes.]*
	If he be married.	
	My grave is like to be my wedding bed.	
Nurse	His name is Romeo, and a Montague;	135
	The only son of your great enemy.	
Juliet	My only love sprung from my only hate!	
	Too early seen unknown, and known too late.	
	Prodigious birth of love it is to me,	
	That I must love a loathèd enemy.	140
Nurse	What's this? what's this?	
Juliet	A rhyme I learned even now	
	Of one I danced withal.	

[Someone calls within, "Juliet!".]

Nurse	Anon, anon!	
	Come let's away, the strangers all are gone.	*Exit all.* 144

134 My grave is like to be my wedding bed: two possible meanings: 1) I'll die unmarried, for I won't marry anyone else; 2) I'll die if I can't marry him

137 sprung from my only hate: born into my enemy's family

138 Too early seen unknown ... too late: I fell in love before I knew who he was

139 Prodigious: unlucky, ominous

143 Anon: I'm on my way

144 strangers: people who don't live in the house

Director's Note, 1.5

✔ Disguised, Romeo and his friends join the dancing.

✔ Tybalt recognises Romeo, is stopped from attacking him by Capulet, and swears vengeance.

✔ Romeo and Juliet meet, and start to fall in love. Later they both discover the other is from the 'enemy' family.

✔ Do we respond differently to their meeting because we know that their love is doomed?

exam PREPARATION

Text focus: Act 1 Scene 5 lines 73–110

• Shakespeare creates mood and atmosphere in differing ways. What characters say and do and even the structure of their language help to create the mood of the scene. Remember to state the mood. Writing "This creates mood" or "This creates an atmosphere" will not gain you marks as you have not said what the mood is. Remember that the mood may not stay constant throughout an extract. Be aware of subtle shifts in atmosphere. Identify the language that shows you this and comment on its effect.

In this scene, Shakespeare chooses to show the lovers meeting in a public situation that embodies the tensions between the feuding families. The fact that the ball goes on while the audience listen in to private conversations shows the public context for personal feelings.

(AO1) Response to characters and events:

• Capulet and Tybalt react differently to spotting Romeo. *How does Shakespeare show this from their language?*

• Capulet is calm at first, but when Tybalt challenges him a different Capulet emerges. *Which words suggest that he is capable of vicious anger if not obeyed?*

• Shakespeare shows us the risk Romeo has taken in coming to the ball. *What effect does he create by his choice of the order of events: Romeo seeing Juliet, Tybalt's quarrel with Capulet, and then Romeo and Juliet's first meeting?*

• Romeo's image of himself as a pilgrim, worshipping at the shrine of Juliet's beauty, continues the idea of courtly love. *Is Romeo's love for Juliet the same as, or different from, his love for Rosaline?*

(AO2) Language, structure and form:

• Tybalt's antagonism reminds us that in Verona, hatred and feuding can erupt at any time. *Why might Shakespeare have put this moment next to Romeo and Juliet's first meeting?*

• Romeo and Juliet's first conversation in lines 92–105 is in the form of a Shakespearean sonnet. Together, the two lovers' lines complete the sonnet. *Why do you think that Shakespeare has done this?*

• The sonnet is full of religious imagery. *Find examples and comment on what they show about Romeo and Juliet's feelings for each other.*

• There is a sensuality about Romeo and Juliet's kiss that suggests the possibility of eventual physical love. *What sort of mood is created here?*

• The lovers' conversation is full of wonder and emotion. *How will this positive atmosphere change when Romeo asks "What is her mother?"*

Question:

How does Shakespeare create mood and atmosphere in this scene? (15 marks)

ACT 2 SCENE 1

Enter Chorus

Chorus

Now old desire doth in his death-bed lie,
And young affection gapes to be his heir.
That fair for which love groaned for and would die,
With tender Juliet matched, is now not fair.
Now Romeo is beloved and loves again,   5
Alike bewitched by the charm of looks,
But to his foe supposed he must complain,
And she steal love's sweet bait from fearful hooks.
Being held a foe, he may not have access
To breathe such vows as lovers use to swear;   10
And she as much in love, her means much less
To meet her new-belovèd any where.
But passion lends them power, time means to meet,
Temp'ring extremities with extreme sweet.

[Exit.]

1 **Now old desire doth in his death-bed lie:** Romeo's old love is dying and his new love waits eagerly to take over
3 **That fair:** Rosaline
4 **matched:** compared
5 **is beloved and loves again:** is in love and loved in return
6 **Alike:** both (Romeo and Juliet)
7 **his foe supposed:** someone who should be his enemy
7 **complain:** beg for love
10 **use to:** normally
11 **her means much less:** has even fewer chances
14 **Temp'ring extremities with extreme sweet:** making the difficulties lighter by the joy of meeting

ACT 2 SCENE 1

Enter Romeo alone.

Romeo

Can I go forward when my heart is here?
Turn back, dull earth, and find thy centre out.

1 **go forward:** walk away
2 **dull earth:** my body
2 **thy centre:** his heart, with Juliet

Enter Benvolio with Mercutio. Romeo hides.

Benvolio

Romeo! My cousin Romeo! Romeo!

Mercutio

He is wise,
And on my life hath stol'n him home to bed.   5

Benvolio

He ran this way and leapt this orchard wall.
Call, good Mercutio.

Mercutio

                Nay, I'll conjure too.
Romeo! Humours! Madman! Passion! Lover!
Appear thou in the likeness of a sigh,
Speak but one rhyme and I am satisfied;   10
Cry but "Ay me", pronounce but " love" and "dove";
Speak to my gossip Venus one fair word,
One nickname for her purblind son and heir,
Young Abraham Cupid, he that shot so trim,
When King Cophetua loved the beggar-maid. –   15
He heareth not, he stirreth not, he moveth not,
The ape is dead, and I must conjure him. –
I conjure thee by Rosaline's bright eyes,
By her high forehead and her scarlet lip,
By her fine foot, straight leg and quivering thigh,   20
And the demesnes that there adjacent lie,
That in thy likeness thou appear to us.

7 **conjure too:** magic him out of the air
8 **Humours:** moody one
9 **likeness:** shape
12 **my gossip:** my good friend (usually said by a woman about another woman)
12 **Venus:** the goddess of love
13 **purblind son and heir:** Venus' son, Cupid
14 **Abraham:** trickster, con-man
15 **King Cophetua:** a king who, in a song, fell in love with and married a socially very unsuitable beggar
17 **The ape is dead:** Romeo is playing dead like a performing monkey
17 **conjure him:** magic him back to life
21 **the demesnes:** places
21 **adjacent:** nearby

Benvolio

And if he hear thee, thou wilt anger him.

Mercutio

This cannot anger him. 'Twould anger him

	To raise a spirit in his mistress' circle,
	Of some strange nature, letting it there stand
	Till she had laid it and conjured it down.
	That were some spite. My invocation
	Is fair and honest, and in his mistress' name
	I conjure only but to raise up him.

Benvolio
Come, he hath hid himself among these trees
To be consorted with the humorous night.
Blind is his love and best befits the dark.

Mercutio
If love be blind, love cannot hit the mark.
Now will he sit under a medlar tree
And wish his mistress were that kind of fruit
As maids call medlars when they laugh alone.
O Romeo that she were, O that she were
An open arse and thou a poperin pear.
Romeo, good night. I'll to my truckle-bed,
This field-bed is too cold for me to sleep.
Come, shall we go?

Benvolio
Go, then; for 'tis in vain
To seek him here that means not to be found.

Exit Mercutio and Benvolio.

ACT 2 SCENE 2

Romeo steps out.

Romeo
He jests at scars that never felt a wound!
But, soft, what light through yonder window breaks?
It is the east and Juliet is the sun
Arise fair sun and kill the envious moon,
Who is already sick and pale with grief
That thou, her maid, art far more fair than she.
Be not her maid! Since she is envious
Her vestal livery is but sick and green

[Enter Juliet above.]

And none but fools do wear it. Cast it off!
It is my lady, O it is my love!
O that she knew she were!
She speaks, yet she says nothing. What of that?
Her eye discourses, I will answer it. –
I am too bold, 'tis not to me she speaks.
Two of the fairest stars in all the heaven,
Having some business, do entreat her eyes
To twinkle in their spheres till they return.
What if her eyes were there, they in her head?
The brightness of her cheek would shame those stars
As daylight doth a lamp. Her eyes in heaven
Would through the airy region stream so bright
That birds would sing and think it were not night.
See how she leans her cheek upon her hand.
O that I were a glove upon that hand,

Line numbers: 25, 30, 35, 40, 5, 10, 15, 20

25 raise a spirit: magic up a spirit but also starts a series of sexual double meanings, in this case 'have an erection'

28 That were some spite: that would be infuriating

28 invocation: conjuring spell

32 To be consorted: be alone with

32 humorous: double meaning: damp; moody

34 the mark: what it aims at

35 medlar: an apple-like fruit, often compared to a vagina

39 open arse: nickname for a medlar

39 poperin pear: a type of pear shaped like a penis

40 truckle-bed: a small pull-out bed, often used by children

Director's Note, 2.1

✔ Romeo hides from his friends, climbing into the Capulets' orchard.

✔ Mercutio and Benvolio look for him, joking about Rosaline.

✔ They give up, and go away.

1 He jests at scars that never felt a wound: only someone who hasn't been in love can joke about the pain it gives

2 soft: hush

6 her maid: Juliet is a virgin and Diana, the moon goddess, also represents chastity

7 Be not her maid: give up your virginity

8 vestal livery: clothes worn by virgins who serve Diana in her temples

11 O that: if only

13 discourses: speaks volumes

16 some business: something they must do

16 do entreat: have begged

17 in their spheres: in their place in the sky

18 there: in the sky

18 they: the stars

21 through the airy region stream: shine in the sky**

That I might touch that cheek.

Juliet   Ay me.

Romeo   She speaks!   25
O speak again, bright angel, for thou art
As glorious to this night, being o'er my head,
As is a wingèd messenger of heaven   28 **wingèd messenger of heaven:** angel
Unto the white-upturnèd wond'ring eyes
Of mortals that fall back to gaze on him   30
When he bestrides the lazy puffing clouds,
And sails upon the bosom of the air.

Juliet   O Romeo, Romeo, wherefore art thou Romeo?   33 **wherefore art thou:** why are you
Deny thy father and refuse thy name,   34 **Deny thy father and refuse thy name:** say you are not a Montague
Or if thou wilt not, be but sworn my love   35
And I'll no longer be a Capulet.

Romeo   *[Aside.]*   Shall I hear more, or shall I speak at this?

Juliet   'Tis but thy name that is my enemy.
Thou art thyself, though not a Montague.   39 **Thou art thyself, though not a Montague:** change your name and you will be the same person
What's Montague? it is nor hand, nor foot,   40
Nor arm, nor face, nor any other part
Belonging to a man. O be some other name!
What's in a name? That which we call a rose
By any other name would smell as sweet.

exam SKILLS

Target skill: analysing the presentation of a relationship

Question: How does Shakespeare present Romeo and Juliet's relationship in Act 2 Scene 2?

Consider the purpose of this scene in the play.
This is a scene where, despite the physical distance between the two lovers (Juliet is above on the balcony), there is an intimacy between them which is shared by the audience. In a strict society which prevented unmarried young men and women from spending time alone together, Shakespeare has presented an opportunity for the lovers to talk secretly. Their relationship moves quickly. By the end of this scene, their intent to marry has been discussed and the action of the play results from this decision.

Consider our opinion of Romeo at this point in the play. Mercutio's exclamatory description of Romeo is still ringing in the ears of the audience – "Romeo! Humours! Madman! Passion! Lover!" and we wonder how many of these names still apply to him. He has been impulsive in entering the dangerous but concealing darkness of the Capulet orchard and is clearly willing to take risks.

Look specifically at the language in this scene.

- Shakespeare has Romeo use images of light to convey his admiration of Juliet. *Find examples and comment on what they reveal abut Romeo's feelings.*
- Juliet's words are filled with both hope and hopelessness. *Find evidence of both.*
- Romeo is anxious to swear his love and Juliet is anxious to prevent such swearing. *What differences in attitude do you notice between the characters?*
- Juliet fears that their "contract" is "too rash, too ill-advised, too sudden". *Why might Shakespeare have given her these words at this point?*

	So Romeo would, were he not Romeo called,	45
	Retain that dear perfection which he owes	
	Without that title. Romeo, doff thy name,	
	And for that name which is no part of thee	
	Take all myself.	

Romeo   I take thee at thy word.
       Call me but love, and I'll be new baptized.   50
       Henceforth I never will be Romeo.

Juliet   What man art thou that thus bescreened in night
       So stumblest on my counsel?

52 **bescreened in:** hidden by
53 **counsel:** private exploration of my thoughts

Romeo   By a name
       I know not how to tell thee who I am.
       My name, dear saint, is hateful to myself,   55
       Because it is an enemy to thee.
       Had I it written, I would tear the word.

Juliet   My ears have not yet drunk a hundred words
       Of thy tongue's uttering, yet I know the sound.
       Art thou not Romeo, and a Montague?   60

59 **Of thy tongue's uttering:** you have spoken

Romeo   Neither, fair maid, if either thee dislike.

61 **if either thee dislike:** if you don't like either of them

Juliet   How camest thou hither, tell me, and wherefore?
       The orchard walls are high and hard to climb,
       And the place death, considering who thou art,
       If any of my kinsmen find thee here.   65

64–5 **the place death … find thee here:** as you are a Montague, any Capulet who finds you here will kill you

Romeo   With love's light wings did I o'erperch these walls,
       For stony limits cannot hold love out,
       And what love can do that dares love attempt.
       Therefore thy kinsmen are no stop to me.

66 **o'erperch:** fly over
67 **stony limits:** walls

Juliet   If they do see thee, they will murder thee.   70

Romeo   Alack, there lies more peril in thine eye
       Than twenty of their swords. Look thou but sweet,
       And I am proof against their enmity.

71 **there lies more peril in thine eye:** your eyes are more dangerous
73 **proof against their enmity:** safe from their hatred

Juliet   I would not for the world they saw thee here.

Romeo   I have night's cloak to hide me from their eyes,   75
       And but thou love me, let them find me here.
       My life were better ended by their hate,
       Than death proroguèd, wanting of thy love.

76 **but:** unless

78 **proroguèd:** postponed
78 **wanting:** lacking

Juliet   By whose direction found'st thou out this place?

Romeo   By love, that first did prompt me to inquire,   80
       He lent me counsel and I lent him eyes.
       I am no pilot, yet, wert thou as far
       As that vast shore washed with the farthest sea,
       I would adventure for such merchandise.

81 **lent me counsel:** advised me
82 **pilot:** navigator that guides ships into harbour
84 **I would adventure for such merchandise:** I'd take the risks with you as the reward
86 **Else:** otherwise

Juliet   Thou know'st the mask of night is on my face,   85
       Else would a maiden blush bepaint my cheek
       For that which thou hast heard me speak to-night.
       Fain would I dwell on form, fain, fain deny
       What I have spoke. But farewell compliment.

88 **Fain would I dwell on form:** I wish we could follow the usual rules of courtship
89 **farewell compliment:** it's too late for those social conventions now

A

Romeo and Juliet, spring 2009.

How well does the actors' body language here fit their words on page 39?

James Alexandrou, Lorraine Burroughs

Dost thou love me? I know thou wilt say "Ay",
And I will take thy word. Yet if thou swear'st,
Thou mayst prove false. At lovers' perjuries
They say Jove laughs. O gentle Romeo,
If thou dost love, pronounce it faithfully.
Or if thou think'st I am too quickly won,
I'll frown and be perverse and say thee nay,
So thou wilt woo. But else, not for the world.
In truth, fair Montague, I am too fond,
And therefore thou mayst think my haviour light.
But trust me, gentleman, I'll prove more true
Than those that have more coying to be strange.
I should have been more strange, I must confess,
But that thou overhcard'st, ere I was ware,
My true love's passion. Therefore pardon me,
And not impute this yielding to light love
Which the dark night hath so discoverèd.

Romeo Lady, by yonder blessed moon I vow,
That tips with silver all these fruit-tree tops —

Juliet O, swear not by the moon, th' inconstant moon,
That monthly changes in her circled orb,
Lest that thy love prove likewise variable.

Romeo What shall I swear by?

Juliet   Do not swear at all.
Or, if thou wilt, swear by thy gracious self,
Which is the god of my idolatry,
And I'll believe thee.

Romeo   If my heart's dear love —

Juliet Well, do not swear. Although I joy in thee,
I have no joy of this contract to-night.
It is too rash, too unadvised, too sudden,
Too like the lightning, which doth cease to be
Ere one can say "It lightens." Sweet, good night.
This bud of love, by summer's ripening breath,
May prove a beauteous flower when next we meet.
Good night, good night, as sweet repose and rest
Come to thy heart as that within my breast.

Romeo O wilt thou leave me so unsatisfied?

Juliet What satisfaction canst thou have tonight?

Romeo Th' exchange of thy love's faithful vow for mine.

Juliet I gave thee mine before thou didst request it.
And yet I would it were to give again.

Romeo Wouldst thou withdraw it? For what purpose love?

Juliet But to be frank, and give it thee again.
And yet I wish but for the thing I have:
My bounty is as boundless as the sea,
My love as deep, the more I give to thee
The more I have, for both are infinite.

92 perjuries: broken oaths
93 Jove: king of the gods in Roman myths
93 laughs: doesn't take them seriously, won't punish them
94 pronounce it faithfully: tell me so truthfully
96 say thee nay: turn you away
97 So thou wilt woo: to keep you courting me
98 fond: infatuated
97 haviour light: behaviour too easy
101 have more coying to be strange: act more distant just to draw you in
102 strange: reserved
103 ere I was ware: before I realised you were there
105–6 And not impute this … discoverèd: and don't think I'm immoral because of what I've said when I thought I was alone

109 inconstant: ever changing
110 in her circled orb: as she moves through the sky

114 of my idolatory: I worship

117 this contract: these promises we are making
118 too unadvised: not thought through

125 unsatisfied: double meaning: without having sorted things out; sexually unsatisfied

129 I would it were to give again: I wish I still had it to give as I choose

131 frank: open and generous

133 my bounty: my willingness to give

90

95

100

105

110

115

120

125

130

135

39

Juliet has a kind of maturity that Romeo lacks. I'm thinking about the Balcony Scene, she controls the events in a way that he doesn't. He allows himself to get carried away with his feelings. If you look at his language in the Balcony Scene he uses huge imagery, he is a king of using big images to describe his feelings. When he is in the orchard, and he looks up at the balcony: 'the moon' and 'the sun' and 'the stars'; he uses the biggest images he can think of to describe his feelings, which is very lovely. It has actually been quite an interesting thing to explore in rehearsals, because the temptation with that kind of language is to get all flowery with it, but actually it's the danger and the pitfall you don't want to fall into. So he's using this large, rather metaphorical language and Juliet's quite practical really. I mean she does say, 'you were the God of my idolatry', which is a massive image to think about. But she's really practical, like, 'if you really love me, let's get married tomorrow'. She takes control in a way that Romeo seems unable to. And whether that says something about her understanding of life and the way one is responsible for one's actions, I'm not sure.

SHAKESPEARE'S WORLD

◇◇◇◇◇◇◇◇◇◇◇

Upper Level

The actors in the open air playhouses used more than just the stage. A trapdoor gave them access to the stage from underneath. There was also an upper level, at the same height as the middle gallery of audience members.

The upper level was small and often crowded. The most expensive seats in the playhouse were up there and the musicians also used it. For this reason, scenes in the upper level are usually very short, and have no more than three actors. Despite these restrictions, Shakespeare and his contemporaries often wrote action for the upper level. This scene is longer than usual, but Juliet is alone and barely has to move. The use of the upper level means that she is both safe at home and at the same time visible to Romeo, who refers to her as 'being o'er my head'. In this way, the upper level allows for an extended moment of intimacy.

Juliet and Romeo. Left: summer 2009; right: 2013.

Both photos were taken at about the same point in the text on page 41 or 42. Which lines do you think were being spoken? As well as giving the line or lines, explain why you chose them.

l Ellie Kendrick, Adetomiwa Edun; *r* Jade Anouka, Will Featherstone

I hear some noise within. Dear love, adieu. —

[Nurse calls within.]

Anon, good nurse! – Sweet Montague, be true.
Stay but a little, I will come again.   *[Exit Juliet above.]*

Romeo   O blessèd, blessèd night! I am afeard
Being in night, all this is but a dream,   140
Too flattering-sweet to be substantial.

[Enter Juliet above.]

Juliet   Three words, dear Romeo, and good night indeed,
If that thy bent of love be honourable,
Thy purpose marriage, send me word tomorrow,
By one that I'll procure to come to thee,   145
Where and what time thou wilt perform the rite,
And all my fortunes at thy foot I'll lay
And follow thee my lord throughout the world.

Nurse   *[Within.]*   Madam!

Juliet   I come, anon.— But if thou mean'st not well,   150
I do beseech thee —

Nurse   *[Within.]*   Madam!

Juliet   By and by, I come.—
To cease thy strife, and leave me to my grief,
Tomorrow will I send.

Romeo   So thrive my soul

Juliet   A thousand times good night!   155

Romeo   A thousand times the worse to want thy light.

Exit Juliet, above.

Love goes toward love as schoolboys from their books,
But love from love, toward school with heavy looks.

Enter Juliet, above, again.

Juliet   Hist, Romeo, hist! O, for a falc'ner's voice,
To lure this tassel-gentle back again.   160
Bondage is hoarse and may not speak aloud,
Else would I tear the cave where Echo lies
And make her airy tongue more hoarse than mine,
With repetition of my Romeo.

Romeo   It is my soul that calls upon my name.   165
How silver-sweet sound lovers' tongues by night,
Like softest music to attending ears.

Juliet   Romeo.

Romeo   My nyas.

Juliet   What o'clock tomorrow
Shall I send to thee?

Romeo   By the hour of nine.

---

137 **Anon:** I'm on my way
138 **Stay but a little:** wait just a minute

141 **flattering-sweet:** perfectly in tune with what I want
141 **substantial:** real

143 **thy bent of love:** your intentions
144 **Thy purpose:** your aim
145 **procure:** set up
146 **the rite:** the wedding ceremony

150 **thou mean'st not well:** you don't mean marriage, just seduction
151 **beseech:** beg
152 **By and by:** right away
153 **thy strife:** trying to make me love you
153 **leave me to my grief:** grief because he doesn't mean to marry her

156 **the worse to want thy light:** darker without you to light it

159 **Hist:** an attention-getting noise, used by a falconer to attract his birds. This starts a series of comparisons with falconry
160 **tassel-gentle:** male falcon
161 **Bondage is hoarse:** prisoners (she's shut in her father's house) must whisper
162 **Echo:** a nymph in Greek mythology who, when her love was rejected, lived in a cave, only able to 'echo' the last words of anything said to her
167 **attending:** listening
168 **nyas:** a young hawk, not yet trained

FROM THE REHEARSAL ROOM...

MAGNETS

Using the Working Cut text, explore how Romeo and Juliet feel about each other in this scene.

- In pairs, read the exchange aloud.
- Now stand opposite each other. Read the extract again, but this time take one step forward if you feel your character is leading, one step backwards if you feel your character is retreating.
- Repeat the exercise several times before discussing what you have discovered about the character's intentions in this scene.

1 Which character is leading in this scene? Find evidence in the text to support your opinion.

2 What does this scene reveal about Romeo and Juliet's feelings for each other?

3 What impact does the Nurse have? How do her interruptions affect the audience?

Working Cut – text for experiment

Jul	I hear some noise within. Dear love, adieu. — *[Nurse calls.]* Anon, good nurse! — Sweet Montague, be true. Stay but a little, I will come again. *[Exit Juliet above.]*
Rom	O blessèd, blessèd night! *[Enter Juliet above.]*
Jul	Three words, dear Romeo, and good night indeed, If that thy bent of love be honourable, Thy purpose marriage, send me word tomorrow, And all my fortunes at thy foot I'll lay And follow thee my lord throughout the world.
Nur	*[Within.]* Madam!
Jul	I come, anon. — But if thou mean'st not well, I do beseech thee —
Nurse	*[Within.]* Madam!
Jul	By and by, I come. — To cease thy strife, and leave me to my grief, To-morrow will I send. A thousand times good night!
Rom	A thousand times the worse to want thy light.
Jul	Hist, Romeo, hist! Romeo. What o'clock tomorrow Shall I send to thee?
Rom	By the hour of nine.
Jul	I will not fail, 'tis twenty years till then.

Juliet	I will not fail, 'tis twenty years till then. I have forgot why I did call thee back.	170
Romeo	Let me stand here till thou remember it.	
Juliet	I shall forget, to have thee still stand there, Rememb'ring how I love thy company.	
Romeo	And I'll still stay, to have thee still forget, Forgetting any other home but this.	
Juliet	'Tis almost morning, I would have thee gone. And yet no further than a wanton's bird, Who lets it hop a little from his hand, Like a poor prisoner in his twisted gyves, And with a silken thread plucks it back again, So loving-jealous of his liberty.	175 180
Romeo	I would I were thy bird.	
Juliet	Sweet, so would I, Yet I should kill thee with much cherishing. Good night, good night! Parting is such sweet sorrow, That I shall say good night till it be morrow.	185
Romeo	*[Exit Juliet, above.]* Sleep dwell upon thine eyes, peace in thy breast, Would I were sleep and peace, so sweet to rest. Hence will I to my ghostly Friar's close cell, His help to crave, and my dear hap to tell.	190

178 **wanton's bird:** spoilt child's pet bird
180 **gyves:** chains that bind his feet
183 **I would:** I wish
184 **much cherishing:** too much attention
189 **Hence will I:** I'll go from here
189 **ghostly Friar's close cell:** the private place of Friar Lawrence, Romeo's 'spiritual' father
190 **crave:** ask for
190 **my dear hap:** my good luck

Director's Note, 2.2

✔ Romeo hides in the Capulets' garden.
✔ He overhears Juliet declare her love for him, and tells her he loves her.
✔ They talk, and despite Juliet's worry that things are moving so fast, agree to marry the next day.
✔ Romeo is to arrange it, and Juliet will send somebody for a message at nine o'clock.
✔ How does Shakespeare show the intensity of their feelings for each other?

ACT 2 SCENE 3

Enter Friar Lawrence, with a basket.

Friar Lawrence The grey-eyed morn smiles on the frowning night,
Check'ring the eastern clouds with streaks of light,
And fleckled darkness, like a drunkard, reels
From forth day's pathway made by Titan's wheels.
Now, ere the sun advance his burning eye,   5
The day to cheer and night's dank dew to dry,
I must upfill this osier cage of ours
With baleful weeds and precious-juicèd flowers.
The earth, that's nature's mother, is her tomb.
What is her burying grave, that is her womb.   10
And from her womb children of divers kind
We sucking on her natural bosom find.
Many for many, virtues excellent,
None but for some, and yet all different.
O mickle is the powerful grace that lies   15
In plants, herbs, stones, and their true qualities.
For nought so vile that on the earth doth live
But to the earth some special good doth give.
Nor aught so good but strained from that fair use,
Revolts from true birth, stumbling on abuse.   20
Virtue itself turns vice, being misapplied,
And vice sometime by action dignified.

Enter Romeo.

Within the infant rind of this weak flower
Poison hath residence and medicine power.
For this, being smelt, with that part cheers each part,   25
Being tasted, slays all senses with the heart.
Two such opposèd kings encamp them still
In man as well as herbs, grace and rude will.
And where the worser is predominant,
Full soon the canker death eats up that plant.   30

Romeo Good morrow, father.

Friar Lawrence   *Benedicite.*
What early tongue so sweet saluteth me?
Young son, it argues a distempered head
So soon to bid good morrow to thy bed.
Care keeps his watch in every old man's eye,   35
And where care lodges, sleep will never lie,
But where unbruisèd youth with unstuffed brain
Doth couch his limbs, there golden sleep doth reign.
Therefore thy earliness doth me assure
Thou art up-roused by some distemp'rature.   40
Or if not so, then here I hit it right,
Our Romeo hath not been in bed tonight.

Romeo That last is true, the sweeter rest was mine.

Friar Lawrence God pardon sin! Wast thou with Rosaline?

Romeo With Rosaline, my ghostly father? No,   45
I have forgot that name and that name's woe.

Friar Lawrence That's my good son, but where hast thou been then?

---

2 **Check'ring:** patterning
3 **fleckled darkness, like a drunkard:** the darkness, streaked with red like a drunkard's face
4 **From forth day's pathway ... wheels:** out of the way of the sun god's chariot and the arrival of day
5 **ere:** before
7 **upfill this osier cage:** fill my willow basket
8 **baleful weeds:** poisonous herbs
9–10 **The earth, that's nature's mother ... is her womb:** the earth is both a burying place and a place that gives plants life
11 **divers kind:** different sorts
13–4 **Many for many ... all different:** many have many uses; none have no use at all
15 **mickle:** great
15 **grace:** healing qualities
17–8 **For nought ... special good doth give:** there's nothing that doesn't have some good to it
19 **aught:** different sorts
19 **strained from that fair use:** used wrongly
20 **Revolts from ... stumbling on abuse:** has a bad effect far from its natural effect
22 **by action dignified:** can be used for a good purpose
23 **infant rind:** undeveloped skin
25 **with that part:** with its smell
26 **slays all senses with the heart:** kills you
28 **grace:** goodness
28 **rude will:** selfish actions
30 **canker:** plant-destroying worm
31 **Benedicite:** God bless you
33 **argues a distempered head:** suggests something is troubling you
35 **Care keeps his watch ... old man's eye:** it is usually the old who lie awake worrying
37 **unbruisèd:** as yet unharmed by life
37 **unstuffed:** not yet over-filled
38 **couch his limbs:** sleep
39 **assure:** convince
40 **up-roused by some distemp'rature:** out of bed because you're troubled
43 **the sweeter rest was mine:** I was doing something better than sleeping
45 **ghostly father:** spiritual father, religious teacher
46 **that name's woe:** the misery it gave me

43

Colin Hurley
The Friar, spring 2009

I find it helpful to look at the story just from my character's point of view. I was in my cell; Romeo turned up and asked me to marry him to Juliet. Because, quite often we don't take into account what we don't know. I didn't witness their meeting.
I don't know whether it's true love or an infatuation, and that's quite important. Having spent what seems like quite a long time trying to talk Romeo down, just calm him down a bit, suddenly I turn and say 'do you know what, I am going to marry you'. A lecture we had was so enlightening in terms of how high the stakes are. What they are doing is a criminal act. The Friar is saying, 'yeah, let's break the law'.

Friar Lawrence and Romeo, 2013.

Friar Lawrence is speaking, and both men's body language is truculent, yet all the lines in this section rhyme. Why might Shakespeare have chosen (unusually) to use rhyme here?

Dickon Tyrrell, Will Featherstone

exam PREPARATION

Text focus: Act 2 Scene 3 lines 57–94

This is the first time we meet Friar Lawrence. In a character essay, it is useful to use the plan outline:
- when the audience is introduced to the character
- their personal qualities
- main events that involve this character.

You can use Act 2 Scene 3 to address the first bullet point and begin to gather points for the second two. Romeo and Juliet's love has developed so rapidly that they already intend to marry without their parents' permission.

Shakespeare slows the pace of the play at the opening of this scene with Friar Lawrence talking about plants, herbs and the nature of life. His knowledge of drugs is important later in the play.

(AO1) Response to characters and events:
- Friar Lawrence thinks Romeo's love for Juliet is too

sudden. *What does he mean by "Young men's love then lies/Not truly in their hearts, but in their eyes"?*
- The Friar has a careful, wise manner. *What advice does he give to Romeo in this scene?*
- The Friar warns "they stumble that run fast" but then agrees to marry Romeo and Juliet surprisingly quickly. *What might his motives be?*

(AO2) Language, structure and form:
- The Friar enjoys using the image of wasted salt tears at Romeo's expense. *Is his mockery justified?*
- Love, in its different forms, is a major theme. *How does Shakespeare use the Friar's mockery to tell the audience more about the theme of love?*

Question:
- How does Shakespeare present Friar Lawrence in Act 2 Scene 3?

Romeo	I'll tell thee, ere thou ask it me again.
	I have been feasting with mine enemy,
	Where on a sudden one hath wounded me 50
	That's by me wounded. Both our remedies
	Within thy help and holy physic lies.
	I bear no hatred, blessèd man, for lo,
	My intercession likewise steads my foe.
Friar Lawrence	Be plain, good son, and homely in thy drift, 55
	Riddling confession finds but riddling shrift.
Romeo	Then plainly know my heart's dear love is set
	On the fair daughter of rich Capulet.
	As mine on hers, so hers is set on mine,
	And all combined, save what thou must combine 60
	By holy marriage. When and where and how
	We met, we wooed and made exchange of vow,
	I'll tell thee as we pass. But this I pray,
	That thou consent to marry us today.
Friar Lawrence	Holy Saint Francis, what a change is here! 65
	Is Rosaline, that thou didst love so dear,
	So soon forsaken? Young men's love then lies
	Not truly in their hearts, but in their eyes.
	Jesu Maria, what a deal of brine
	Hath washed thy sallow cheeks for Rosaline! 70
	How much salt water thrown away in waste
	To season love, that of it doth not taste.
	The sun not yet thy sighs from heaven clears,
	Thy old groans yet ringing in my ancient ears.
	Lo here upon thy cheek the stain doth sit 75
	Of an old tear that is not washed off yet.
	If e'er thou wast thyself, and these woes thine,
	Thou and these woes were all for Rosaline.
	And art thou changed? Pronounce this sentence then,
	Women may fall, when there's no strength in men. 80
Romeo	Thou chid'st me oft for loving Rosaline.
Friar Lawrence	For doting, not for loving, pupil mine.
Romeo	And bad'st me bury love.
Friar Lawrence	Not in a grave,
	To lay one in, another out to have.
Romeo	I pray thee, chide me not. Her I love now 85
	Doth grace for grace, and love for love allow.
	The other did not so.
Friar Lawrence	O she knew well
	Thy love did read by rote, that could not spell.
	But come young waverer, come, go with me,
	In one respect I'll thy assistant be. 90
	For this alliance may so happy prove,
	To turn your households' rancour to pure love.
Romeo	O let us hence. I stand on sudden haste.
Friar Lawrence	Wisely and slow, they stumble that run fast. *Exit both.*

51–2 **Both our remedies ... holy physic lies:** you can cure us both by helping us and using your religious powers
54 **intercession:** the thing I ask for
54 **likewise steads:** also helps
55 **Be plain:** make your meaning clear
55 **homely in thy drift:** use simple language
56 **Riddling confession finds but riddling shrift:** your confession has to be properly understood to be properly pardoned
63 **pass:** walk along
67 **forsaken:** abandoned
69 **brine:** tears
70 **sallow** sickly-looking
72 **season:** give flavour
75 **Lo:** look
77 **thou wast thyself, and these woes thine:** you were telling the truth about how you felt
79 **Pronounce this sentence then:** then this is my verdict
80 **Women may fall ... strength in men:** when men are weak, what chance do women have
81 **chid'st:** were angry with me
82 **doting:** being infatuated
84 **To lay one in, another out to have:** to bury one love in and take another from
86 **grace for grace, and love for love allow:** loves me equally
88 **read by rote, that could not spell:** just going through the motions, not real
90 **In one respect:** for one reason
91 **this alliance:** their marriage
92 **rancour:** deep-rooted enmity
93 **I stand on sudden haste:** I'm in a hurry

Director's Note, 2.3

✓ Romeo goes straight to Friar Lawrence.
✓ Friar Lawrence assumes Romeo has been with Rosaline, so Romeo tells him he now loves Juliet, and the couple want the Friar to marry them.
✓ Friar Lawrence points out Romeo's love changes very quickly, but agrees to marry them.
✓ Why does Friar Lawrence agree to marry them?

ACT 2 SCENE 4

Enter Benvolio and Mercutio.

Mercutio Where the devil should this Romeo be?
Came he not home tonight?

Benvolio Not to his father's, I spoke with his man.

Mercutio Why that same pale hard-hearted wench, that Rosaline,
Torments him so, that he will sure run mad.

Benvolio Tybalt, the kinsman of old Capulet,
Hath sent a letter to his father's house.

Mercutio A challenge, on my life.

Benvolio Romeo will answer it.

Mercutio Any man that can write may answer a letter.

Benvolio Nay, he will answer the letter's master how he dares, being dared.

Mercutio Alas poor Romeo, he is already dead: stabbed with a white wench's black eye, run through the ear with a love song, the very pin of his heart cleft with the blind bow-boy's butt-shaft. And is he a man to encounter Tybalt?

Benvolio Why, what is Tybalt?

Mercutio More than prince of cats. O he's the courageous captain of compliments. He fights as you sing prick-song, keeps time, distance and proportion. Rests me his minim rests, one, two, and the third in your bosom. The very butcher of a silk button, a duellist, a duellist, a gentleman of the very first house, of the first and second cause. Ah, the immortal *passado*, the *punto reverso*, the *hay*.

Benvolio The what?

Mercutio The pox of such antic, lisping, affecting fantasticoes, these new tuners of accent! "By Jesu, a very good blade! A very tall man! A very good whore!" Why, is not this a lamentable thing, grandsire, that we should be thus afflicted with these strange flies, these fashion-mongers, these pardon-me's, who stand so much on the new form, that they cannot sit at ease on the old bench? O their bones, their bones!

Enter Romeo.

Benvolio Here comes Romeo, here comes Romeo.

Mercutio Without his roe, like a dried herring. O flesh, flesh, how art thou fishified? Now is he for the numbers that Petrarch flowed in: Laura to his lady was but a kitchen wench (marry, she had a better love to be-rhyme her), Dido a dowdy; Cleopatra a gipsy; Helen and Hero hildings and harlots; Thisbe a grey eye or so, but not to the purpose. Signior Romeo, *bonjour*. There's a

---

1 **should:** can
7 **his father's:** Romeo's father's
8 **A challenge, on my life:** I bet it is a challenge to a duel
9 **answer:** accept
11 **how he dares, being dared:** if he really will fight having issued the challenge
15 **pin of his heart:** heart's centre
15 **cleft:** split
15–6 **the blind bow-boy's:** Cupid's
16 **butt-shaft:** blunt, target practice arrow
16 **encounter:** fight a duel with
17 **what is:** what kind of a man is
18 **prince of cats:** refers to Tybert, prince of cats in a well-known story at the time
19 **captain of compliments:** master of all the latest rules of fighting
19–20 **sing prick-song:** sight read sheet music; start of a run of comparisons between duelling and singing.
22 **The very butcher of a silk button:** he could cut your coat buttons off
23 **of the very first house:** from the best school of fencing
23–4 **of the first and second cause:** the two acceptable reasons for duelling
24–5 ***passado* ... *hay*:** fencing terms
27–8 **the pox of ... tuners of accent:** curse these affected people with their put on accents (he then imitates them)
29 **tall:** brave
30 **grandsire:** grandfather
31 **strange flies:** foreign insects
31 **fashion-mongers:** slaves to the latest thing in speech and dress
32 **pardon-me's:** over-polite people
32 **stand so:** insist on
33 **form:** double meaning: bench; behaviour
33 **old bench:** old ways of behaving
36 **roe:** double meaning: female deer; semen. The start of a run of double meanings implying Romeo has had sex
37–8 **for the numbers ... flowed in:** he'll write classical love poetry, like the Roman poet Petrarch to his mistress Laura
40–1 **Dido ... Cleopatra ... Helen ... Hero ... Thisbe:** all women in great love stories

	French salutation to your French slop. You gave us the counterfeit fairly last night.
Romeo	Good morrow to you both. What counterfeit did I give you?
Mercutio	The slip, sir, the slip. Can you not conceive?
Romeo	Pardon, good Mercutio, my business was great, and in such a case as mine a man may strain courtesy.
Mercutio	That's as much as to say, such a case as yours constrains a man to bow in the hams.
Romeo	Meaning, to courtesy.
Mercutio	Thou hast most kindly hit it.
Romeo	A most courteous exposition.
Mercutio	Nay, I am the very pink of courtesy.
Romeo	Pink for flower.
Mercutio	Right.
Romeo	Why, then is my pump well flowered.
Mercutio	Sure wit, follow me this jest now till thou hast worn out thy pump, that when the single sole of it is worn, the jest may remain after the wearing, solely singular.
Romeo	O single-soled jest, solely singular for the singleness.
Mercutio	Come between us, good Benvolio, my wits faint.
Romeo	Switch and spurs, switch and spurs, or I'll cry a match.
Mercutio	Nay, if our wits run the wild-goose chase, I am done. For thou hast more of the wild-goose in one of thy wits than, I am sure, I have in my whole five. Was I with you there for the goose?
Romeo	Thou wast never with me for anything when thou wast not there for the goose.
Mercutio	I will bite thee by the ear for that jest.
Romeo	Nay, good goose, bite not.
Mercutio	Thy wit is a very bitter sweeting, it is a most sharp sauce.
Romeo	And is it not then well served into a sweet goose?
Mercutio	O here's a wit of cheveril, that stretches from an inch narrow to an ell broad!
Romeo	I stretch it out for that word "broad", which added to the goose, proves thee far and wide a broad goose.
Mercutio	Why, is not this better now than groaning for love? Now art thou sociable, now art thou Romeo, now art thou what thou art, by art as well as by nature. For this drivelling love is like a great natural that runs lolling up and down to hide his bauble in a hole.
Benvolio	Stop there, stop there.

Line numbers: 45, 50, 55, 60, 65, 70, 75, 80

43 **French slop:** baggy breeches
43–4 **gave us the counterfeit:** tricked us

47 **the slip:** double meaning: fake coin; avoiding them
47 **conceive:** work out what I mean
49 **strain courtesy:** be rude

50–1 **such a case ... in the hams:** you're so tired from sex you're weak at the knees

53 **Thou hast most kindly hit it:** that's right

56 **Pink:** a garden flower; 'flower' was used to refer to virginity, male and female
58 **is my pump well flowered:** double meaning: well decorated dancing shoe; loss of virginity (deflowering)
60 **single:** only; Romeo and Mercutio start a battle of puns about wearing out shoes and sex being wearing
63 **Come between us:** stop us punning
64 **Switch and spurs ... cry a match:** you have to try harder, as a rider forces a horse on with a whip and spurs, or I've won
65 **wild-goose chase:** triple meaning: the horse racing equivalent of follow-my-leader; 'goose' was slang for both 'prostitute' and 'fool'
67–8 **Was I with you there for the goose?:** did I keep up now I've started goose puns?
73 **sweeting:** apple used for apple sauce
75–6 **here's a wit ... an ell broad:** you can make your small wit stretch a long way
77 **broad:** double meaning: wide; indecent
81 **by art:** because you're quick witted again
82 **drivelling:** talking nonsense
82 **a great natural:** a simple-minded person
83 **bauble:** double meaning: jester's blown-up pig's bladder; penis
85 **tale:** double meaning: story; sounds like 'tail', slang for penis. More puns on this follow

ACT 2 SCENE 4

Mercutio	Thou desirest me to stop in my tale against the hair.	85
Benvolio	Thou wouldst else have made thy tale large.	
Mercutio	O, thou art deceived; I would have made it short, for I was come to the whole depth of my tale, and meant, indeed, to occupy the argument no longer.	

Enter Nurse and Peter.

Romeo	Here's goodly gear. A sail, a sail!	90
Mercutio	Two, two, a shirt and a smock.	
Nurse	Peter!	
Peter	Anon.	
Nurse	My fan, Peter.	
Mercutio	Good Peter, to hide her face! For her fan's the fairer face!	95
Nurse	God you good morrow, gentlemen.	
Mercutio	God you good e'en, fair gentlewoman.	
Nurse	Is it good e'en?	
Mercutio	'Tis no less, I tell you, for the bawdy hand of the dial is now upon the prick of noon.	100
Nurse	Out upon you! What a man are you?	
Romeo	One, gentlewoman, that God hath made, himself to mar.	
Nurse	By my troth, it is well said; "for himself to mar", quoth a? Gentlemen, can any of you tell me where I may find the young Romeo?	105
Romeo	I can tell you. But young Romeo will be older when you have found him than he was when you sought him. I am the youngest of that name, for fault of a worse.	
Nurse	You say well.	
Mercutio	Yea, is the worst well? Very well took, i' faith, wisely, wisely.	110
Nurse	If you be he, sir, I desire some confidence with you.	
Benvolio	She will endite him to some supper.	
Mercutio	A bawd, a bawd, a bawd. So ho!	
Romeo	What hast thou found?	115
Mercutio	No hare, sir; unless a hare, sir, in a Lenten pie that is something stale and hoar ere it be spent.	
	[*Sings.*] An old hare hoar,	
	And an old hare hoar,	
	Is very good meat in Lent.	120
	But a hare that is hoar	
	Is too much for a score,	
	When it hoars ere it be spent.	
	Romeo, will you come to your father's? We'll to dinner thither.	125

85 against the hair: double meaning: against my wish; sounds like 'hare', slang for prostitute

90 goodly gear: new material for joking
90 a sail!: a sailor's cry on seeing a ship
91 a shirt and a smock: a man and a woman

96 God you good morrow: Good morning
97 e'en: any time after noon

99 bawdy: sexually explicit
99 dial: sundial

101 Out upon you: for shame
101 What a man: what kind of a man
102 mar: ruin

103 By my troth: truly
103–4 quoth a?: he says

108 for the fault of a worse: for lack of anything worse

110 took: understood
112 confidence: private conversation; Shakespeare has the Nurse misuse words as part of the comedy of the scene – she may mean for 'conference'
113 endite: deliberate mistake for 'invite'
114 bawd: woman who runs a brothel
114 So ho!: a hunting call
116–23 No hare, sir ... ere it be spent: Mercutio mocks the nurse, obscenely punning on her age, the similarity in sound between 'hoar' and 'whore' and the fact 'hare' was slang for prostitute

124 dinner: the midday meal

Romeo	I will follow you.
Mercutio	Farewell, ancient lady. Farewell lady, lady, lady.

Exit Mercutio and Benvolio.

Nurse I pray you, sir, what saucy merchant was this, that was so full of his ropery?

Romeo A gentleman, nurse, that loves to hear himself talk and will speak more in a minute than he will stand to in a month. 130

Nurse An a speak anything against me, I'll take him down, and a' were lustier than he is, and twenty such jacks. And if I cannot, I'll find those that shall. Scurvy knave, 135 I am none of his flirt-gills; I am none of his skains-mates. *[To Peter.]* And thou must stand by too, and suffer every knave to use me at his pleasure?

Peter I saw no man use you at his pleasure. If I had, my weapon should quickly have been out, I warrant you, I dare 140 draw as soon as another man, if I see occasion in a good quarrel, and the law on my side.

Nurse Now, afore God, I am so vexed that every part about me quivers. Scurvy knave! *[To Romeo.]* Pray you, sir, a word. And as I told you, my young lady bid me enquire 145 you out. What she bid me say, I will keep to myself. But first let me tell ye, if ye should lead her into a fool's paradise, as they say, it were a very gross kind of behaviour, as they say. For the gentlewoman is young, and therefore, if you should deal double with her, truly 150 it were an ill thing to be offered to any gentlewoman, and very weak dealing.

Romeo Nurse, commend me to thy lady and mistress. I protest unto thee —

Nurse Good heart, and i' faith, I will tell her as much. Lord, 155 Lord, she will be a joyful woman.

Romeo What wilt thou tell her, nurse? Thou dost not mark me.

Nurse I will tell her, sir, that you do protest which, as I take it, is a gentlemanlike offer.

Romeo Bid her devise some means to come to shrift this 160 afternoon, and there she shall at Friar Lawrence's cell be shrived and married. *[He offers her money.]* Here is for thy pains.

Nurse No truly sir; not a penny.

Romeo Go to, I say you shall. 165

Nurse This afternoon, sir? Well, she shall be there.

Romeo And stay, good nurse, behind the abbey wall.
Within this hour my man shall be with thee
And bring thee cords made like a tackled stair,
Which to the high topgallant of my joy 170

128 **saucy merchant:** rude, un-gentlemanly man
129 **ropery:** spiteful and sexual jokes

131 **stand to:** put up with
133 **An a:** and if he
133 **take him down:** take him down a peg or two
134 **lustier:** stronger
134 **jacks:** yobs
135 **Scurvy knave:** discourteous villain
136-7 **flirt-gills, skains-mates:** whores
138 **suffer:** allow
138 **use me at his pleasure:** take advantage of me (unintentional double meaning)

147-8 **lead her into a fool's paradise:** promise marriage only to seduce her
148 **gross:** monstrous
150 **deal double:** deceive
152 **weak dealing:** shameful behaviour
153 **commend me:** give my greetings to
153-4 **I protest unto thee:** I assure you

157 **mark:** listen to

160 **devise some means:** find a way to
160 **shrift:** confession, where she tells her sins to a Catholic priest or friar
161-2 **be shrived:** have her sins forgiven

169 **cords made like a tackled stair:** a rope ladder
170 **the high topgallant of my joy:** Juliet's balcony

	Must be my convoy in the secret night. Farewell, be trusty and I'll quit thy pains. Farewell, commend me to thy mistress.	171 **convoy:** way up 172 **quit thy pains:** reward your efforts
Nurse	Now God in heaven bless thee. Hark you, sir.	
Romeo	What sayest thou, my dear nurse? 175	
Nurse	Is your man secret? Did you ne'er hear say, Two may keep counsel putting one away?	176 **secret:** able to keep a secret 177 **Two may keep counsel … away:** Proverb: two can keep a secret; three can't 178 **Warrant thee:** I promise
Romeo	Warrant thee, my man's as true as steel.	
Nurse	Well, sir; my mistress is the sweetest lady. Lord, Lord, when 'twas a little prating thing. — O, there is a 180 nobleman in town, one Paris, that would fain lay knife aboard. But she, good soul, had as lief see a toad, a very toad, as see him. I anger her sometimes and tell her that Paris is the properer man, but I'll warrant you, when I say so, she looks as pale as any clout in 185 the 'versal world. Doth not rosemary and Romeo begin both with a letter?	180 **prating:** chattering 181-2 **would fain lay knife aboard:** wants to marry her 182 **as lief:** rather 184 **properer:** handsomer 185 **as pale as any clout:** a common saying 186 **'versal:** whole 186 **rosemary:** herb of remembrance, used at weddings and funerals
Romeo	Ay, nurse, what of that? Both with an R.	
Nurse	Ah, mocker, that's the dog's name. R is for the — No, I know it begins with some other letter, and she hath the 190 prettiest sententious of it, of you and rosemary, that it would do you good to hear it.	189 **dog's name:** 'r' sounds like growling 191 **sententious:** she means 'sentence', for saying
Romeo	Commend me to thy lady. *[Exit Romeo.]*	
Nurse	Ay, a thousand times. — Peter.	
Peter	Anon. 195	
Nurse	Before and apace. *Exit Nurse and Peter.*	196 **Before and apace:** go in front and hurry

Enter Juliet.

Juliet The clock struck nine when I did send the nurse,
In half an hour she promised to return.
Perchance she cannot meet him. That's not so.   **3 Perchance:** perhaps
O, she is lame. Love's heralds should be thoughts,   **4 heralds:** messengers
Which ten times faster glide than the sun's beams   5
Driving back shadows over louring hills.   **6 louring:** dark, threatening
Therefore do nimble-pinioned doves draw Love,   **7 Therefore do .... draw Love:**
And therefore hath the wind-swift Cupid wings.   that's why swift-winged doves
Now is the sun upon the highmost hill   pull the chariot of Venus (the
Of this day's journey, and from nine till twelve   10   goddess of love)
Is three long hours, yet she is not come.
Had she affections and warm youthful blood,
She would be as swift in motion as a ball.
My words would bandy her to my sweet love,   **14 bandy:** hit her (like a tennis ball)
And his to me.   15
But old folks, many feign as they were dead,   **16 feign as:** act as if
Unwieldy, slow, heavy, and pale as lead.

Enter Nurse and Peter.

O God, she comes! O honey nurse, what news?
Hast thou met with him? Send thy man away.

Nurse Peter, stay at the gate.   *[Exit Peter.]* 20 **20 stay:** wait

Juliet Now good sweet nurse — O Lord, why look'st thou sad?
Though news be sad, yet tell them merrily.
If good, thou shamest the music of sweet news
By playing it to me with so sour a face.

Nurse I am a-weary, give me leave awhile.   25 **25 give me leave awhile:** just wait
Fie, how my bones ache! What a jaunce have I had!   a minute
                                                         26 jaunce: exhausting trip

Juliet I would thou hadst my bones, and I thy news.
Nay, come I pray thee, speak good, good nurse, speak.

Nurse Jesu, what haste! Can you not stay awhile?
Do you not see that I am out of breath?   30

Juliet How art thou out of breath, when thou hast breath
To say to me that thou art out of breath?
The excuse that thou dost make in this delay   **34 thou dost excuse:** you say you
Is longer than the tale thou dost excuse.   have no breath to tell
Is thy news good, or bad? Answer to that.   35
Say either, and I'll stay the circumstance.   **36 stay the circumstance:** wait for
Let me be satisfied, is't good or bad?   the details

Nurse Well, you have made a simple choice. You know   **38 simple:** foolish
not how to choose a man. Romeo? No, not he, though
his face be better than any man's, yet his leg excels all 40 **42 be not to be talked on:** aren't
men's, and for a hand, and a foot, and a body, though   worth talking about
they be not to be talked on, yet they are past compare.   **43 the flower of courtesy:** perfect
He is not the flower of courtesy, but I'll warrant him   in his manners
as gentle as a lamb. Go thy ways, wench. Serve God. —   **44 Go thy ways, wench. Serve**
What, have you dined at home?   45   **God:** but that's enough of that, be
                                                             a good girl

51

A   B   C

exam PREPARATION

Text focus: Act 2 Scene 5 lines 45–77

Include the question in the opening paragraph of your answer, to show the examiner that you are engaging with what you have been asked to look at.

(AO1) Response to characters and events:

- Juliet's frustration at the lack of information is apparent. By saying "O God's lady dear, Are you so hot?" and "bear the burden soon at night" the Nurse reminds us that Juliet is longing to be with Romeo. *How are these comments typical of the Nurse's attitude to love?*
- The Nurse enjoys the delay in giving Juliet news from Romeo. Her self-interruption – "Where is your Mother?" – reminds us of the difference between Juliet's relationship with her mother and the Nurse. *How do the relationships differ?*
- Juliet often acts quite maturely in the play but seems to behave more true to her age here. *Why do you think this is?*

(AO2) Language, structure and form:

- The structure of the dialogue emphasises the contrasting feelings of Juliet and the Nurse: one desperate for information; the other determined not to reveal that information until she is ready. *Find evidence that Juliet is both frustrated with the Nurse and grateful to her for bringing her news.*
- The tone of the Nurse's words changes noticeably at line 66 – "Have you got leave to go to shrift today?" From then on it is positive and purposeful. *Find examples of the Nurse's instructions to Juliet and comment on their effect.*
- Tensions between youth and age are one of the play's themes. The theme is serious when linked to the Capulets' ignorance of their daughter's plans. Here, the theme is presented humorously between Juliet and the Nurse. *How does Shakespeare use humour here to show the differences between youth and age?*

Question: How does Shakespeare present the relationship between Juliet and the Nurse at this stage of the play? (15 marks)

Juliet	No, no. But all this did I know before. What says he of our marriage? What of that?
Nurse	Lord, how my head aches! What a head have I! It beats as it would fall in twenty pieces. My back a' t' other side. Ah, my back, my back! Beshrew your heart for sending me about To catch my death with jauncing up and down.
Juliet	I' faith, I am sorry that thou art not well. Sweet, sweet, sweet nurse, tell me what says my love?
Nurse	Your love says, like an honest gentleman, And a courteous, and a kind, and a handsome, And I warrant a virtuous — Where is your mother?
Juliet	Where is my mother? Why, she is within, Where should she be? How oddly thou repliest. "Your love says, like an honest gentleman, Where is your mother?"
Nurse	O God's lady dear, Are you so hot? Marry, come up, I trow. Is this the poultice for my aching bones? Henceforward do your messages yourself.
Juliet	Here's such a coil. Come, what says Romeo?
Nurse	Have you got leave to go to shrift to-day?
Juliet	I have.
Nurse	Then hie you hence to Friar Lawrence's cell, There stays a husband to make you a wife. Now comes the wanton blood up in your cheeks, They'll be in scarlet straight at any news. Hie you to church, I must another way, To fetch a ladder by the which your love Must climb a bird's nest soon when it is dark. I am the drudge and toil in your delight, But you shall bear the burden soon at night. Go, I'll to dinner, hie you to the cell.
Juliet	Hie to high fortune! Honest nurse, farewell.

Exit Juliet and Nurse.

50
55
60
65
70
75

50 **a' t' other side:** on the other side
51 **Beshrew:** curse
52 **jauncing:** prancing like a horse
55 **honest:** honourable
58 **within:** indoors
61 **God's lady dear:** Mary, Christ's mother
62 **hot:** impatient
62 **Marry, come up, I trow:** exclamation of impatience
63 **poultice:** soothing warm pack of herbs
64 **Henceforward:** from now on
65 **coil:** fuss
66 **shrift:** confession, where she tells her sins to a Catholic priest
68 **hie you hence:** go
70 **wanton:** passionate
75 **drudge:** poor, unimportant servant
76 **bear the burden:** carry the weight of Romeo during sex

Director's Note, 2.5

✔ Juliet waits impatiently for the Nurse to return.

✔ The Nurse teases Juliet, complaining about how tired the errand has made her.

✔ She finally tells Juliet the arrangements to meet Romeo and be married.

✔ What moods does Shakespeare create in this scene?

Actor's view

Ellie Kendrick
Juliet, summer 2009

The soliloquy at the beginning is fantastic because it is just a 13-year-old girl speaking. All teenagers remember that time when they are desperately waiting for a call, or really excited about the person they have got a crush on. But, obviously, with Juliet it is really quite exaggerated. And, so I think it is a really lovely soliloquy, and it is very humorous as well, when she is mocking old folks being, 'slow, heavy, and pale as lead'.

It is a classic teenagers' speech, not sympathising with the elders, and resenting the Nurse for failing to come quick enough to deliver the message from her loved one. And I think it is very clear that she knows the Nurse very well in this scene, because she is very frustrated with her, we can see that in lines when she says:

"How art thou out of breath, when thou hast breath
To say to me that thou art out of breath?"

(Which in itself is a line which is very difficult to say with enough breath.) So she is clearly irritated with her, but there is a huge amount of affection there, and she also knows that she has to flatter the Nurse in order to get the information she wants out of her. So she says, throughout the scene, 'Sweet, sweet, sweet nurse,' 'honey nurse' and really sucks up to her. So on the one side there is that, on the other side she is getting really frustrated with her for failing to tell her the news that she wants to hear.

exam SKILLS

Target skill: assessing the importance of a scene

Shakespeare crafted the plot carefully. You need to show that you understand the key purpose of each scene. Order the points below from most to least important, to explain why this short scene is so significant.

- People at the time thought secret marriages were wrong and there are just three people there.
- Showing them before the marriage but not the marriage itself saves time and means the plot can move more quickly.
- The scene underlines the strong sexual attraction between Romeo and Juliet – that's why Lawrence says "you shall not stay alone".
- It keeps the tension high – the original audiences didn't know if something would stop the marriage.

Juliet and Romeo kiss during Act 2 Scene 6, 2004.

1 There is no stage direction for a kiss in this scene. Why do you think the director and actors chose to add one? Explain your reasons, quoting from the text to support your answer if you can.

2 If you were the director, when would you have Juliet and Romeo kiss? Explain why.

Kananu Kirimi, Tom Burke

Enter Friar Lawrence and Romeo.

Friar Lawrence	So smile the heavens upon this holy act,
	That after hours with sorrow chide us not!
Romeo	Amen, amen. But come what sorrow can,
	It cannot countervail the exchange of joy
	That one short minute gives me in her sight.
	Do thou but close our hands with holy words,
	Then love-devouring death do what he dare,
	It is enough I may but call her mine.
Friar Lawrence	These violent delights have violent ends
	And in their triumph, die like fire and powder,
	Which as they kiss consume. The sweetest honey
	Is loathsome in his own deliciousness,
	And in the taste confounds the appetite.
	Therefore love moderately, long love doth so,
	Too swift arrives as tardy as too slow.

Juliet runs in and embraces Romeo.

	Here comes the lady. O so light a foot
	Will ne'er wear out the everlasting flint.
	A lover may bestride the gossamers
	That idles in the wanton summer air,
	And yet not fall, so light is vanity.
Juliet	Good even to my ghostly confessor.
Friar Lawrence	Romeo shall thank thee, daughter, for us both.
Juliet	As much to him, else is his thanks too much.
Romeo	Ah, Juliet, if the measure of thy joy
	Be heaped like mine, and that thy skill be more
	To blazon it, then sweeten with thy breath
	This neighbour air, and let rich music's tongue
	Unfold the imagined happiness that both
	Receive in either by this dear encounter.
Juliet	Conceit, more rich in matter than in words,
	Brags of his substance, not of ornament.
	They are but beggars that can count their worth,
	But my true love is grown to such excess
	I cannot sum up sum of half my wealth.
Friar Lawrence	Come, come with me, and we will make short work.
	For, by your leaves, you shall not stay alone
	Till holy church incorporate two in one.

[Exit Friar, Romeo and Juliet.]

2 **after hours with sorrow chide us not:** we aren't punished by sorrow in the future
4 **countervail:** equal
6 **Do thou but ... holy words:** Just marry us
10 **powder:** gunpowder
11 **as they kiss consume:** burn each other up on touching
12 **Is loathsome in his own deliciousness:** can be sickly because it is so delicious
13 **confounds:** spoils
15 **tardy:** late
17 **ne'er:** never
17 **the everlasting flint:** the ground
18 **bestride the gossamers:** walk so lightly on spiders' webs
19 **idles:** drift
20 **vanity:** the delights of the world
21 **ghostly:** spiritual
21 **confessor:** priest or friar who hears a person confess their sins
24–5 **the measure of thy joy Be heaped like mine:** if you're as happy as I am
25 **that:** if
26 **blazon:** describe
27 **This neighbour air:** the air around us
28 **Unfold:** tell
28–9 **both Receive in either:** we both will have
30–1 **Conceit, more rich ... of ornament:** understanding boasts about what it really has, it doesn't dress it up in fancy words
32 **They are but beggars ... worth:** only beggars can list all they have
34 **sum up sum:** calculate
35 **make short work:** quickly marry you
37 **incorporate two in one:** has made you husband and wife

Director's Note, 2.6

✔ Friar Lawrence and Romeo wait for Juliet.
✔ She arrives, and Friar Lawrence takes them off to marry them.
✔ Why might Shakespeare have included this short scene?

ACT 3 SCENE 1

SHAKESPEARE'S WORLD

Sword fighting

A sword was part of an Elizabethan gentleman's elaborate dress. Most gentlemen carried swords in public, and many had a dagger too. The weapons were more a sign of status than for defence. However, young gentlemen, or gallants as they were known, did fight in the streets. The fact that even the servants in *Romeo and Juliet* carry swords, and shields too (not normally carried at all), is a sign of just how extreme the old feud has become.

Gentlemen were taught the art of fencing. In this scene, Mercutio uses fencing terms and also complains that Tybalt 'fights by the book'. The fights themselves were governed by a strict set of rules that they were honour bound to obey. Tybalt breaks these rules by thrusting under Romeo's arm.

The open air playhouses did more than just show plays. They staged exhibitions of sword fighting, tournaments and prize fights between duellers. Some theatres including The Curtain, where *Romeo and Juliet* was probably first played, became well known for these fights. With the exciting swordplay of the first half of the play, Shakespeare is giving his audience the action they expect, as well as the main plot of the love story.

ACT 3 SCENE 1

Enter Benvolio, Mercutio, his page, and servants of the Montagues.

Benvolio	I pray thee, good Mercutio, let's retire,	
	The day is hot, the Capels are abroad,	
	And if we meet we shall not 'scape a brawl,	
	For now these hot days is the mad blood stirring.	
Mercutio	Thou art like one of those fellows, that when he enters	5
	the confines of a tavern, claps me his sword upon the	
	table and says "God send me no need of thee", and	
	by the operation of the second cup, draws him on the	
	drawer, when indeed there is no need.	
Benvolio	Am I like such a fellow?	10
Mercutio	Come, come, thou art as hot a Jack in thy mood as any	
	in Italy, and as soon moved to be moody, and as soon	
	moody to be moved.	
Benvolio	And what to?	
Mercutio	Nay, and there were two such, we should have none	15
	shortly, for one would kill the other. Thou? Why thou	
	wilt quarrel with a man that hath a hair more, or a hair	
	less, in his beard than thou hast. Thou wilt quarrel with	
	a man for cracking nuts, having no other reason but	
	because thou hast hazel eyes. What eye but such an eye,	20
	would spy out such a quarrel? Thy head is as full of	
	quarrels as an egg is full of meat, and yet thy head hath	
	been beaten as addle as an egg for quarrelling. Thou	
	hast quarrelled with a man for coughing in the street,	
	because he hath wakened thy dog that hath lain asleep	25
	in the sun. Didst thou not fall out with a tailor for	
	wearing his new doublet before Easter? With another,	
	for tying his new shoes with old ribbon? And yet thou	
	wilt tutor me from quarrelling?	

1 **retire:** go home
2 **Capels:** Capulets
2 **abroad:** somewhere around
3 **'scape a brawl:** be able to avoid a fight

6 **the confines of a tavern:** a pub
6 **claps me his sword:** bangs his sword
8 **the operation of the second cup:** the time he's had his second drink
8 **draws him:** draws his sword
9 **drawer:** man serving the drink
11 **hot:** quick-tempered
11 **Jack:** fellow
12–3 **as soon moved to be moody ... moved:** as quickly made angry as you are made angry that it has happened
15 **and there were:** if there were

20 **hazel:** double meaning: eye colour; type of nut

22 **meat:** something edible
23 **addle:** rotten (so an egg that won't produce a chick)

27 **doublet:** jacket

29 **tutor me from:** advise me to avoid

Benvolio	And I were so apt to quarrel as thou art, any man should buy the fee-simple of my life for an hour and a quarter.	30
Mercutio	The fee-simple? O simple!	

Enter Tybalt, Petruchio, and others.

Benvolio	By my head, here comes the Capulets.	
Mercutio	By my heel, I care not.	35
Tybalt	*[To his men.]* Follow me close, for I will speak to them. *[To Benvolio and Mercutio.]* Gentlemen, good-e'en, a word with one of you.	
Mercutio	And but one word with one of us? Couple it with something, make it a word and a blow.	
Tybalt	You shall find me apt enough to that, sir, and you will give me occasion.	40
Mercutio	Could you not take some occasion without giving?	
Tybalt	Mercutio, thou consortest with Romeo.	
Mercutio	Consort? What, dost thou make us minstrels? And thou make minstrels of us, look to hear nothing but discords. *[Moving his hand to his sword.]* Here's my fiddlestick, here's that shall make you dance. 'Zounds, consort!	45
Benvolio	We talk here in the public haunt of men. Either withdraw unto some private place, Or reason coldly of your grievances, Or else depart. Here all eyes gaze on us.	50
Mercutio	Men's eyes were made to look, and let them gaze. I will not budge for no man's pleasure, I. *[Enter Romeo.]*	
Tybalt	Well, peace be with you, sir, here comes my man.	
Mercutio	But I'll be hanged, sir, if he wear your livery. Marry, go before to field, he'll be your follower. Your worship in that sense may call him "man."	55
Tybalt	Romeo, the love I bear thee can afford No better term than this: thou art a villain.	
Romeo	Tybalt, the reason that I have to love thee Doth much excuse the appertaining rage To such a greeting. Villain am I none, Therefore farewell, I see thou knowest me not.	60
Tybalt	Boy, this shall not excuse the injuries That thou hast done me, therefore turn and draw.	65
Romeo	I do protest I never injured thee, But love thee better than thou canst devise Till thou shalt know the reason of my love. And so, good Capulet, which name I tender As dearly as my own, be satisfied.	70
Mercutio	O calm, dishonourable, vile submission! *Alla stoccata* carries it away. *[Drawing his sword.]*	

Glossary

30 **And I were so apt:** if I was so given to
31 **fee-simple:** complete ownership
33 **simple:** fool
34 **By my head:** a common exclamation
35 **By my heel:** Mercutio makes up this exclamation, which hints at running away
38 **Couple:** join
41 **occasion:** a good reason
43 **consortest with:** are a friend of
44 **minstrels:** music makers – 'consort' is a name of a small group of musicians
44 **And thou:** if you
46 **fiddlestick:** he means his sword
47 **'Zounds:** an oath, from 'God's wounds'
48 **the public haunt of men:** a public place
50 **reason coldly of:** calmly talk through
53 **I will not budge for no man's pleasure:** I won't move for any man's convenience
54 **my man:** the man I'm looking for
55 **I'll be hanged, sir, if he wear your livery:** he's certainly not a Capulet's servant ('man' can mean 'servant' who wears his master's 'livery' or uniform)
56 **go before to field:** lead the way to the duelling place
56 **follower:** another word for 'servant' but meaning that Romeo will follow to fight
61–2 **the appertaining rage To such a greeting:** the anger I should feel at such an insult
64 **Boy:** an insult to a young man
65 **turn and draw:** come back and fight
67 **devise:** imagine
69 **tender:** value
70 **be satisfied:** don't push this challenge
72 *Alla stoccata:* another reference to fancy fencing terms

57

exam SKILLS

Target skill: interpreting mood and atmosphere

Question: How does Shakespeare create mood and atmosphere in lines 73–107?

If the extract question asks you to look at how mood and atmosphere are created, you will need to show an understanding of Shakespeare's craft.

- Tybalt wants to fight Romeo rather than Mercutio. *Explain why.*
- The atmosphere is tense before the violence begins. Mercutio responds to Tybalt with questions, insults, threats and references to fencing terms.
- Comment on the effect that you think each of these would have on Tybalt.
- Romeo uses the exclamatory mood when he speaks. *Find examples and comment on his likely state of mind.*
- This a very visual scene with plenty of action onstage. *How would this affect the mood of the scene?*
- The scene is tense but exciting. *How does the mood of excitement change to something more serious from line 88 onwards?*
- The audience knows Mercutio as a humorous character and friend to Romeo, whereas Tybalt has been presented an quarrelsome man. *How does the audience's likely siding with Mercutio affect the mood here?*
- Even when fatally wounded, Mercutio can make jokes as a "grave man", but when he cries "A plague on both your houses" he is deadly serious. *How does this affect the atmosphere of the scene?*

	Tybalt, you rat-catcher, will you walk?	
Tybalt	What wouldst thou have with me?	
Mercutio	Good king of cats, nothing but one of your nine lives, that I mean to make bold withal, and as you shall use me hereafter, drybeat the rest of the eight. Will you pluck your sword out of his pilcher by the ears? Make haste, lest mine be about your ears ere it be out.	75
Tybalt	I am for you. *[Drawing his sword.]*	80
Romeo	Gentle Mercutio, put thy rapier up.	
Mercutio	Come sir, your *passado*. *[They fight.]*	
Romeo	Draw, Benvolio; beat down their weapons. Gentlemen, for shame, forbear this outrage! Tybalt, Mercutio, the Prince expressly hath Forbidden bandying in Verona streets: Hold, Tybalt! good Mercutio!	85

[During the fight, Romeo tries to part them, and Tybalt stabs Mercutio under Romeo's arm. Tybalt runs offstage.]

Mercutio	I am hurt. A plague on both your houses! I am sped. Is he gone and hath nothing?	
Benvolio	What, art thou hurt?	90
Mercutio	Ay, ay, a scratch, a scratch. Marry, 'tis enough. Where is my page? Go, villain, fetch a surgeon. *[Exit Page.]*	
Romeo	Courage man, the hurt cannot be much.	
Mercutio	No, 'tis not so deep as a well, nor so wide as a church door; but 'tis enough, 'twill serve. Ask for me tomorrow, and you shall find me a grave man. I am peppered, I warrant, for this world. A plague o' both your houses! 'Zounds, a dog, a rat, a mouse, a cat to scratch a man to death, a braggart, a rogue, a villain, that fights by the book of arithmetic! — Why the devil came you between us? I was hurt under your arm.	95 100
Romeo	I thought all for the best.	
Mercutio	Help me into some house, Benvolio, Or I shall faint. A plague o' both your houses! They have made worms' meat of me. I have it, and soundly too. Your houses!	105

Exit Mercutio, helped by Benvolio and the servants.

Romeo	This gentleman, the Prince's near ally, My very friend, hath got his mortal hurt In my behalf. My reputation stained With Tybalt's slander, — Tybalt, that an hour Hath been my cousin. O sweet Juliet, Thy beauty hath made me effeminate And in my temper softened valour's steel.	110

73 **will you walk:** will you fight me

76 **to make bold withal:** to take
77 **drybeat:** beat up, rather than fight with swords, like gentlemen
78 **pilcher:** scabbard
78 **by the ears:** right now, with no formality
79 **lest:** in case

82 *passado:* fencing term

84 **forbear:** stop

86 **bandying:** fighting

88 **A plague on both your houses:** curse both Montagues and Capulets
88 **sped:** fatally wounded
89 **Is he gone and hath nothing?:** has Tybalt got away unwounded?
91 **'tis enough:** it's enough to kill me

95 **'twill serve:** it's enough to kill me
96 **grave:** double meaning: serious; dead
97 **peppered:** ruined, finished off

100-1 **by the book of arithmetic:** 'by numbers', by the rules of fencing

106 **worms' meat:** a corpse
107 **I have it, and soundly too:** I'm certainly fatally wounded
108 **near ally:** close relative
109 **very:** true
110 **In my behalf:** defending me
111 **that an hour:** that for an hour
113 **effeminate:** weak, not manly
114 **temper:** double meaning: hardening (as in steel for a sword); nature
114 **softened valour's steel:** made me cowardly

Text focus: Act 3 Scene 1 lines 145–180

(AO1) Response to characters and events:

- Shakespeare created Mercutio as the most joyous character in the play, full of wit, humour and courage. *Why does Shakespeare kill him off at this point in the play?*
- Benvolio does not know the reason for Romeo's earlier reluctance to fight Tybalt, but he still draws attention to Romeo's initial patience. *How does this account encourage the audience's sympathy for Romeo rather than Tybalt?*
- Tybalt's character was set from the start: an implacable enemy of the Montagues, whose hatred was exacerbated by seeing Romeo at the Capulet ball. *Will an audience feel he deserved to die?*
- Family honour is a major concern in the play. *How does Lady Capulet reinforce its significance?*

(AO2) Language, structure and form:

- Lady Capulet's extravagant grief is focused on Tybalt's relationships: he is "cousin", "my brother's child" and "dear kinsman". *Why might Shakespeare have given her so many relationship words?*
- Lady Capulet moves quickly to state "shed blood of Montague." *She is clearly upset, but what does she hope to gain from Tybalt's death?*
- Benvolio's language is considered as he attempts to give an accurate account of events. *Why does Lady Capulet dismiss his account so quickly?*
- Consider the structure of the play. *What is the effect of Shakespeare locating this scene straight after Romeo and Juliet's marriage?*

(AO4) Vocabulary, sentences and spelling:

- Avoid repeating *This shows me…* in your sentence structures. Try: *This illustrates…,/ This suggests….*

Question:

How does Shakespeare present reactions to the death of Mercutio in this extract? (15 marks)

The Prince, Capulet, Lady Capulet, Tybalt (dead) and Benvolio, spring 2009.

1 How have the characters reacted to the death of Tybalt?

2 How might the audience react to his death?

l–r Nick Khan, Vincent Brimble, Golda Rosheuvel, Marshall Griffin, Ben Aldridge

Enter Benvolio.

Benvolio	O Romeo, Romeo, brave Mercutio is dead.	115
	That gallant spirit hath aspired the clouds,	
	Which too untimely here did scorn the earth.	

116-7 That gallant spirit hath aspired ... the earth: his soul has scorned the earth and flown to Heaven too soon

Romeo	This day's black fate on more days doth depend,	
	This but begins the woe others must end.	

118 on more days doth depend: will have an effect on the future

Benvolio	Here comes the furious Tybalt back again. *Enter Tybalt.*	120

119 others: other days

Romeo	Alive in triumph and Mercutio slain?	
	Away to heaven respective lenity,	
	And fire and fury be my conduct now.	
	Now, Tybalt, take the "villain" back again	
	That late thou gav'st me, for Mercutio's soul	125
	Is but a little way above our heads,	
	Staying for thine to keep him company.	
	Either thou, or I, or both, must go with him.	

122 Away to heaven respective lenity: no more treating him like a relative
123 be my conduct: drive my actions
125 late: just now

127 Staying: waiting

Tybalt	Thou wretched boy, that didst consort him here,	
	Shalt with him hence.	

129 that didst consort him: who was with him

Romeo	This shall determine that.	130

They fight. Tybalt falls.

130 Shalt with him hence: will leave with him
130 This: Romeo's sword

Benvolio	Romeo, away, be gone!	
	The citizens are up, and Tybalt slain.	
	Stand not amazed, the Prince will doom thee death	
	If thou art taken. Hence, be gone, away!	

133 amazed: stunned
133 doom thee: sentence you to

Romeo	O! I am fortune's fool!	
Benvolio	Why dost thou stay?	135

Exit Romeo, then enter citizens from another door.

135 fortune's fool: the puppet of Fortune, the goddess of luck

Citizen	Which way ran he that killed Mercutio?	
	Tybalt, that murderer, which way ran he?	
Benvolio	There lies that Tybalt.	
Citizen	Up, sir, go with me.	
	I charge thee in the Prince's name, obey.	

139 charge: order

Enter the Prince, Montague, Capulet, their wives and others.

Prince	Where are the vile beginners of this fray?	140
Benvolio	O noble Prince, I can discover all	
	The unlucky manage of this fatal brawl.	
	There lies the man, slain by young Romeo,	
	That slew thy kinsman, brave Mercutio.	

140 the vile beginners of this fray: those who started this fight
141 discover: tell
142 manage: events

Lady Capulet	Tybalt, my cousin! O my brother's child!	145
	O Prince! O cousin! Husband! O, the blood is spilled	
	Of my dear kinsman. Prince, as thou art true,	
	For blood of ours, shed blood of Montague.	
	O cousin, cousin!	

147 true: fair

Prince	Benvolio, who began this bloody fray?	150

WORDS FAILING

- In groups of five, read lines 140–196, each taking one part.
- Look carefully at Benvolio's description of events to the Prince. Note words and phrases that depict each stage of the fight.
- Compare Benvolio's step-by-step account of the fight with Tybalt and Romeo's exchange in lines 21–30.

1 Is Benvolio telling the truth?

2 What role does Benvolio play in the scene between Romeo and Tybalt?

3 How does Romeo respond to Mercutio's death?

4 How does Romeo react after Tybalt's death?

5 Who is most to blame for Tybalt's death? Find evidence in the text to support your opinion.

Director's view

Dominic Dromgoole
Director, summer 2009

It is hard to deny that Lady Capulet's attachment to Tybalt. I think you can overplay it, and sometimes you see it overplayed in the Ball scene. And even though the actress playing Lady Capulet was always very enthusiastic to get her hands on the actor playing Tybalt, we tried to tamp it down a little bit in that scene. It is very clear the extremity of the reaction is so enormous when Tybalt is dead, and then the degree of her grief is so extended, and so absolute afterwards, it does seem there is more than a familial attachment there. And it is set up very delicately and very well, the fact that there is a dysfunction in the relationship between Capulet and his wife and that that is not as vigorous or as healthy or active as it might be, so it seems that Tybalt is there to step in.

Actor's view

Yolanda Vazquez
Lady Capulet, 2008
(not a Globe production)

I don't think Lady Capulet's reaction to Tybalt's death means she has been having an affair with him. Tybalt is a young man, her brother's son, who she is very close to and loves very much. I have three nephews, if anything would happen to them ... I think that for Lady Capulet, losing Tybalt is like losing the son she never had. She is looking after him. He is part of her household, she is looking after him, which is what they used to do with young men and young women, so she's looking after her brother's son, and he dies in her care.

exam SKILLS

Target skill: analysing Shakespeare's structuring of the play

Question: What might Shakespeare have wanted his audience to be thinking at this point in the play?

Different interpretations of the text are always possible. With a partner, read the pairs of statements below and decide which best represents your thoughts about the play so far. Then make up your own pair of statements. Compare your choices with other pairs.

1 **Either**
The Prologue told us what was going to happen so that took the tension out of watching the play.
or
Although we know what will happen we still care about the characters while we are watching them.

2 **Either**
The young people of Verona are shown as trapped in their feuding families, so responsibility lies with the older generation.
or

Even the young characters in the play are shown as responsible for what they choose to do – they can't just blame their parents.

3 **Either**
Shakespeare constructs a situation where Romeo has to choose between two evils – there is no right way forward for him.
or
Had Shakespeare allowed Romeo to put love before honour, tragedy could have been avoided, but that would have spoilt the play.

4 **Either**
By this point in the play we know that things can only lead to a tragic ending.
or
We can't help hoping that someone (possibly the Friar?) will find a way for Romeo and Juliet to be together.

How do the insights you have gained from this exercise help you answer the question above?

Benvolio   Tybalt, here slain, whom Romeo's hand did slay.
Romeo that spoke him fair, bid him bethink
How nice the quarrel was, and urged withal
Your high displeasure. All this uttered
With gentle breath, calm look, knees humbly bowed,   155
Could not take truce with the unruly spleen
Of Tybalt, deaf to peace, but that he tilts
With piercing steel at bold Mercutio's breast.
Who all as hot, turns deadly point to point
And, with a martial scorn, with one hand beats   160
Cold death aside and with the other sends
It back to Tybalt, whose dexterity
Retorts it. Romeo, he cries aloud,
"Hold, friends! Friends, part!" And swifter than his tongue
His agile arm beats down their fatal points,   165
And 'twixt them rushes, underneath whose arm
An envious thrust from Tybalt hit the life
Of stout Mercutio, and then Tybalt fled.
But by and by comes back to Romeo,
Who had but newly entertained revenge,   170
And to 't they go like lightning, for ere I
Could draw to part them, was stout Tybalt slain.
And as he fell, did Romeo turn and fly.
This is the truth, or let Benvolio die.

Lady Capulet   He is a kinsman to the Montague,   175
Affection makes him false he speaks not true.
Some twenty of them fought in this black strife,
And all those twenty could but kill one life.
I beg for justice, which thou, Prince, must give.
Romeo slew Tybalt, Romeo must not live.   180

Prince   Romeo slew him, he slew Mercutio.
Who now the price of his dear blood doth owe?

Montague   Not Romeo, Prince, he was Mercutio's friend.
His fault concludes but what the law should end,
The life of Tybalt.

Prince   And for that offence   185
Immediately we do exile him hence.
I have an interest in your hate's proceeding,
My blood for your rude brawls doth lie a-bleeding.
But I'll amerce you with so strong a fine
That you shall all repent the loss of mine.   190
I will be deaf to pleading and excuses;
Nor tears nor prayers shall purchase out abuses.
Therefore use none. Let Romeo hence in haste,
Else, when he is found, that hour is his last.
Bear hence this body and attend our will.   195
Mercy but murders, pardoning those that kill.

Exit all, some carrying Tybalt's body.

152 **spoke him fair:** was polite
152 **bethink:** consider
153 **nice:** trivial
153 **withal:** as well
156 **take truce with:** pacify
156 **unruly spleen:** hot temper
157 **but that he tilts:** so that he thrusts
160 **martial:** war-like
162 **dexterity:** skill
166 **'twixt:** between
167 **envious:** malicious
167 **hit the life:** killed

169 **by and by:** at that moment
170 **but newly entertained:** just decided on
171 **ere:** before
172 **draw:** draw my sword
172 **stout:** brave
173 **fly:** run away
176 **Affection makes him false:** he's biased in their favour
177 **black strife:** evil attack
182 **Who now the price of his dear blood doth owe?:** So who should pay for that?
184 **His fault concludes ... should end:** his action (killing Tybalt) was only what your punishment would have been anyway, for killing Mercutio
186 **exile him hence:** send him away from Verona
187 **an interest in your hate's proceeding:** I've become personally involved in your quarrels
188 **My blood:** Mercutio
189 **amerce:** punish
190 **the loss of mine:** the death of my relative
192 **purchase out abuses:** by pardons for these crimes
194 **Else:** otherwise
194 **that hour is his last:** he will be executed
195 **attend our will:** come with me to hear your punishment
196 **Mercy but murders ... kill:** if I pardon murder it will just lead to more killing

Director's Note, 3.1

✔ Tybalt, determined to fight Romeo, meets Mercutio and Benvolio. Romeo arrives, but refuses to fight.
✔ Shocked at Romeo's refusal, Mercutio fights Tybalt and is fatally wounded.
✔ Romeo now wants revenge, and fights and kills Tybalt.
✔ Romeo flees. The Prince arrives and banishes Romeo.

Target skill: analysing language

Question: How does Shakespeare show Juliet's state of mind in lines 1–40?

A character's language and behaviour help to reveal their state of mind. Here, Juliet is excited about spending the night with Romeo. Sshe wants day to pass and "love-performing night" to come. We saw in the balcony scene how candid she was to an unseen Romeo. Now, with characteristic honesty, she admits her eagerness. However, her excitement has turned to panic and concern by the end of the scene.

- There is dramatic irony in this scene as the audience, unlike Juliet, know about Tybalt's death and Romeo's banishment. *How does this affect our reaction to Juliet's soliloquy?*

- List the images that Juliet uses to describe herself, night, love and Romeo. *What impact might these comparisons have on an audience?*
- Shakespeare uses these poetic techniques here:
  - allusion to classical myth ("Phoebus")
  - metaphors ("Spread thy close curtain")
  - alliteration ("sober-suited matron")
  - personification ("loving black-browed night")
  - hyperbole ("all the world will be in love with night.")
  - animal imagery ("Hood my unmanned blood bating in my cheeks")
  How do these techniques tell you more about Juliet's state of mind?
- Although Juliet initially misunderstands the Nurse's news, it still signals a dramatic change in mood. *Which line shows that Juliet's good mood is gone?*

'Enter the Nurse, carrying a rope ladder', 2004.

Look for Shakespeare giving the actors clues about stage directions in the dialogue. By what line should the Nurse have dropped the rope ladder?

Bette Bourne

Enter Juliet alone.

Juliet Gallop apace, you fiery-footed steeds,
      Towards Phoebus' lodging. Such a wagoner
      As Phaeton would whip you to the west,
      And bring in cloudy night immediately.
      Spread thy close curtain, love-performing night, 5
      That runaways' eyes may wink, and Romeo
      Leap to these arms, untalked of and unseen.
      Lovers can see to do their amorous rites
      By their own beauties. Or, if love be blind,
      It best agrees with night. Come civil night, 10
      Thou sober-suited matron all in black,
      And learn me how to lose a winning match,
      Played for a pair of stainless maidenhoods.
      Hood my unmanned blood, bating in my cheeks
      With thy black mantle, till strange love grow bold, 15
      Think true love acted simple modesty.
      Come night, come Romeo, come, thou day in night;
      For thou wilt lie upon the wings of night
      Whiter than new snow on a raven's back.
      Come gentle night, come loving black-browed night. 20
      Give me my Romeo, and when I shall die,
      Take him and cut him out in little stars,
      And he will make the face of heaven so fine
      That all the world will be in love with night,
      And pay no worship to the garish sun 25
      O, I have bought the mansion of a love,
      But not possessed it, and though I am sold,
      Not yet enjoyed. So tedious is this day
      As is the night before some festival
      To an impatient child that hath new robes 30
      And may not wear them. O, here comes my nurse.

Enter the Nurse, carrying a rope ladder.

      And she brings news, and every tongue that speaks
      But Romeo's name speaks heavenly eloquence.
      Now, nurse, what news? What hast thou there, the cords
      That Romeo bid thee fetch?

Nurse   Ay, ay, the cords. 35

Juliet Ay me, what news? Why dost thou wring thy hands?

Nurse Ah, welladay! He's dead, he's dead, he's dead!
      We are undone, lady, we are undone!
      Alack the day, he's gone, he's killed, he's dead.

Juliet Can heaven be so envious?

Nurse   Romeo can, 40
      Though heav'n cannot. O Romeo, Romeo!
      Who ever would have thought it? Romeo!

Juliet What devil art thou that dost torment me thus?
      This torture should be roared in dismal hell.

1–4 **Gallop apace ... night immediately:** Juliet is urging the day to pass quickly using images of Phoebus' (the sun god's) chariot driven by his son, Phaeton

5 **close:** concealing

6 **runaways' eyes may wink:** the eyes of those who are still out may not notice

8 **do their amorous rites:** make love

10 **best agrees:** is most suited to

10 **civil:** respectable

11 **sober-suited matron:** older woman dressed respectably

12 **learn me:** teach me

12 **how to lose a winning match:** how to lose my virginity and win my husband

13 **a pair of stainless maidenheads:** the virginities of Romeo and Juliet

14 **Hood my unmanned ... cheeks:** hide my blushes (falcon imagery of putting a hood over a young, untrained hawk's head to calm it)

15 **black mantle:** the darkness of night

15 **strange:** unfamiliar

16 **Think true love ... modesty:** see sex between true lovers as respectable

25 **garish:** vulgar, over-bright

26–8 **bought the mansion ... Not yet enjoyed:** I'm married in name but not yet a proper wife

33 **But:** only

33 **heavenly eloquence:** the most beautiful language

34 **the cords:** the rope ladder

37 **welladay:** expression of misery

38 **undone:** ruined

40 **envious:** malicious, spiteful

40 **Romeo can:** the nurse knows he's killed Tybalt

44 **this torture:** the nurse's rambling

Juliet, listening to the Nurse, summer 2009.

Look closely at the expression on her face. Which part of which of the Nurse's speeches do you think she is listening to? Quote from the text and explain your answer.

Ellie Kendrick

Actor's view

Lorraine Burroughs
Juliet, spring 2009

Why Juliet chooses Romeo's banishment as more important than Tybalt's death is raw emotion. Tybalt is her cousin and she loves him – it's awful what has happened and her first initial reaction is utter disgrace at Romeo for what he has done and she feels completely betrayed of the love she has given him and how she has opened up to him and said that she is going to give her life to him and he has done that to her and her family. She tries to hate him but she can't, she loves him and the fact that he's banished, everything that they have just gone through is ruined, is going to be worthless if she stays angry with Romeo and that's it, over. She has to address this and find him and figure out how she is going to see him again because he now is her life. Tybalt being alive or dead isn't an issue in comparison to her and Romeo, Romeo is her life, without him she is dead.

Actor's view

Ellie Kendrick
Juliet, summer 2009

Yes, Juliet really goes through a whirlwind of emotions in this scene. She starts with immense joy, very happy, because she is going to be seeing her husband, and that is really exciting for her. And then she goes from that immense joy to sudden, desperate, sadness because she thinks the Nurse is telling her Romeo is dead. But then the Nurse finally says it, very plainly, after going round the houses. She says, 'Tybalt is gone and Romeo banished,/Romeo that killed him, he is banishèd.' And then for Juliet, her instant first reaction is one of immense shock: 'Did Romeo's hand shed Tybalt's blood?' And I played that as her being really shocked and appalled by that, and then she very interestingly manifests this cognitive dissonance which she is feeling, in her speech that follows, when she uses a series of antitheses – 'Beautiful tyrant, fiend angelical … Despisèd substance of divinest show!' And she is using lots of opposites which represent the opposites of feeling that she is having – hate and love for Romeo. But it is not until she hears criticism of Romeo in the Nurse's mouth, 'Shame come to Romeo!' that she suddenly realises how wrong she is, and instantly regrets that huge well of anger that she had against him. And she says, 'Blistered be thy tongue/For such a wish!' to the Nurse, and then goes on to realise that Romeo is everything to her, that she would not care if all her family were dead as long as he is still around.

	Hath Romeo slain himself? Say thou but "Ay",	45
	And that bare vowel "I" shall poison more	
	Than the death-darting eye of cockatrice.	
	I am not I, if there be such an ay.	
	Or those eyes shut, that make thee answer "Ay."	
	If he be slain, say "Ay"; or if not, "No."	50
	Brief sounds determine of my weal or woe.	
Nurse	I saw the wound, I saw it with mine eyes,	
	God save the mark, here on his manly breast.	
	A piteous corse, a bloody piteous corse.	
	Pale, pale as ashes, all bedaubed in blood,	55
	All in gore-blood; I swoonèd at the sight.	
Juliet	O break my heart, poor bankrupt, break at once!	
	To prison, eyes, ne'er look on liberty.	
	Vile earth to earth resign, end motion here.	
	And thou and Romeo press one heavy bier.	60
Nurse	O Tybalt, Tybalt, the best friend I had.	
	O courteous Tybalt, honest gentleman,	
	That ever I should live to see thee dead!	
Juliet	What storm is this that blows so contrary?	
	Is Romeo slaughtered? And is Tybalt dead?	65
	My dearest cousin, and my dearer lord?	
	Then dreadful trumpet sound the general doom,	
	For who is living, if those two are gone?	
Nurse	Tybalt is gone and Romeo banished,	
	Romeo that killed him, he is banishèd.	70
Juliet	O God! Did Romeo's hand shed Tybalt's blood?	
Nurse	It did, it did, alas the day, it did!	
Juliet	O serpent heart, hid with a flowering face.	
	Did ever dragon keep so fair a cave?	
	Beautiful tyrant, fiend angelical,	75
	Ravenous dove-feathered raven! Wolvish-ravening lamb,	
	Despisèd substance of divinest show!	
	Just opposite to what thou justly seem'st,	
	A damnèd saint, an honourable villain.	
	O nature! What hadst thou to do in hell	80
	When thou didst bower the spirit of a fiend	
	In mortal paradise of such sweet flesh?	
	Was ever book containing such vile matter	
	So fairly bound? O that deceit should dwell	
	In such a gorgeous palace!	
Nurse	There's no trust,	85
	No faith, no honesty in men. All perjured,	
	All forsworn, all naught, all dissemblers.	
	Ah, where's my man? Give me some *aqua vitae*!	
	These griefs, these woes, these sorrows make me old.	
	Shame come to Romeo!	
Juliet	Blistered be thy tongue	90
	For such a wish! He was not born to shame.	

45 **Ay:** triple meaning: yes; the pronoun 'I'; sounds like 'eye' (Juliet uses all these in the next few lines)

47 **cockatrice:** a mythical creature whose looks could kill

51 **determine of my weal or woe:** will decide if I am to be happy or miserable

53 **God save the mark:** God forgive me for saying so

54 **piteous corse:** corpse that would fill you with pity

56 **gore-blood:** congealing blood

56 **swoonèd:** fainted

57 **bankrupt:** her heart has lost all it had, as a bankrupt has lost all his money and has to go to prison

59 **Vile earth ... end motion here:** I must die too and be buried in the earth

60 **And thou ... heavy bier:** my body will be carried to the grave with Romeo's

62 **honest:** honourable

64 **so contrary:** in different directions

66 **lord:** husband

67 **dreadful trumpet sound the general doom:** the world has ended, it is the Day of Judgement

73 **serpent:** the serpent that tempted Eve in the Bible story

73 **flowering:** handsome, smiling

74 **keep:** own, live in

76 **Ravenous dove-feathered raven:** greedy raven dressed in a dove's white feathers

76 **Wolvish-ravening lamb:** lamb that behaves like a wolf

77 **Despisèd substance of divinest show:** vile thing that appears so beautiful

78 **justly:** truly, actually

81 **bower the spirit of a fiend:** hide a devil's soul

84 **fairly:** beautifully

86–7 **perjured, forsworn, dissemblers:** liars

88 **man:** servant

88 ***aqua vitae:*** strong alcoholic drink, like brandy

Text focus: Act 3 Scene 2 lines 75–126

An analysis of this scene would fit well in a number of possible essays, including those about Juliet, the Nurse and the themes of love, conflict, loyalty and secrecy.

In this extract, Shakespeare presents Juliet as a daughter of the Capulet family and as a "three-hours wife" in the Montague family – two conflicting roles. Juliet has been on a see-saw of emotions: eager anticipation followed by despair.

(AO1) Response to characters and events

- Juliet begins with her own condemnation of Romeo, then moves to defend him. *What moves her to this seeming change of heart?*
- Juliet speaks at length about how the impact she feels from the word "banishèd" is ten thousand times stronger than Tybalt's death. *What might Shakespeare be saying about the power of words?*
- Shakespeare links the tensions of the wider family feud in Verona to Juliet's emotional dilemma. *What choices does she have at this point of the play?*

(AO2) Language, structure and form

- Juliet's speech is full of impossible opposites such as "fiend angelical, Ravenous dove-feathered raven!" *Shakespeare has given Juliet unusual language here. What is its effect on the audience?*
- Juliet is weeping in line 102, so the image of a river is fitting. She wants the river to reverse its flow from her eyes. *What argument does she use in order to try to lift her mood?*
- Roles and proper names have a high profile in the passage: "husband", "cousin", "father" and "mother", together with the repetition of names – Tybalt, Romeo, Juliet. *Why do you think Shakespeare has Juliet use so many names here?*
- Shakespeare has Juliet use both the exclamatory and imperative mood quite frequently in this extract. *What does this show about her state of mind?*

(AO4) Vocabulary, sentences and spelling:

- Keep developing the way you express your answers. Try: *this conveys / this portrays / which emphasises / accentuates / amplifies the idea of…*

Question: How does Shakespeare present Juliet's conflicting emotions in this scene?

Juliet and the Nurse, 2013

Juliet goes through many emotions in this scene. What might she and the Nurse be concentrating on at this point? Quote from the text to support your answer.

Jade Anouka, Lisa Stevenson

Director's Note, 3.2

✔ Juliet longs for night and Romeo's arrival.

✔ The Nurse arrives, grieving for Tybalt's death.

✔ At first Juliet is confused, and fears Romeo is dead.

✔ When she understands Romeo is banished, she despairs for her marriage.

✔ The Nurse goes to make arrangements for Juliet and Romeo to spend the night together.

✔ How does Juliet's emotional state change during the scene?

Upon his brow shame is ashamed to sit;
For 'tis a throne where honour may be crowned
Sole monarch of the universal earth.   94   **Sole monarch:** absolute ruler
O what a beast was I to chide at him!   95   95   **chide at him:** speak badly of
                                                            him

Nurse   Will you speak well of him that killed your cousin?

Juliet   Shall I speak ill of him that is my husband?
Ah, poor my lord, what tongue shall smooth thy name   98   **smooth thy name:** restore your
When I, thy three-hours wife, have mangled it?   reputation
But, wherefore, villain, didst thou kill my cousin?   100   100   **wherefore:** why
That villain-cousin would have killed my husband.
Back foolish tears, back to your native spring,   102   **native spring:** source, her eyes
Your tributary drops belong to woe,   103   **tributary drops:** tears
Which you mistaking offer up to joy.
My husband lives, that Tybalt would have slain;   105
And Tybalt's dead, that would have slain my husband.
All this is comfort, wherefore weep I then?
Some word there was, worser than Tybalt's death,
That murdered me. I would forget it fain,   109   **forget it fain:** gladly forget it
But O, it presses to my memory   110
Like damnèd guilty deeds to sinners' minds.
"Tybalt is dead, and Romeo banished",
That "banishèd", that one word "banishèd",
Hath slain ten thousand Tybalts. Tybalt's death
Was woe enough if it had ended there.   115
Or if sour woe delights in fellowship   116   **sour woe delights in**
And needly will be ranked with other griefs,   **fellowship:** misery loves
Why followed not, when she said "Tybalt's dead",   company
Thy father or thy mother, nay, or both,   117   **needly will be ranked:** must be
Which modern lamentations might have moved?   120   part of
But with a rear-ward following Tybalt's death,   118   **she:** the nurse
"Romeo is banishèd". To speak that word   120   **modern lamentations might**
Is father, mother, Tybalt, Romeo, Juliet,   **have moved:** would just have
All slain, all dead. "Romeo is banishèd!"   caused normal, ordinary grief
There is no end, no limit, measure, bound,   125
In that word's death. No words can that woe sound.   126   **that word's death:** the death
Where is my father and my mother, Nurse?   that word brings
                                                      126   **sound:** measure

Nurse   Weeping and wailing over Tybalt's corse.
Will you go to them? I will bring you thither.

Juliet   Wash they his wounds with tears, mine shall be spent,   130   130   **spent:** shed
When theirs are dry, for Romeo's banishment.
Take up those cords. Poor ropes, you are beguiled,   132   **beguiled:** cheated
Both you and I, for Romeo is exiled.
He made you for a highway to my bed,
But I, a maid, die maiden-widowèd.   135   135   **maid:** virgin
Come cords, come nurse, I'll to my wedding-bed,   135   **maiden-widowèd:** a virgin and a
And death, not Romeo, take my maidenhead.   widow
                                                      137   **maidenhead:** virginity

Nurse   Hie to your chamber. I'll find Romeo   138   **Hie:** go straight
To comfort you, I wot well where he is.
Hark ye, your Romeo will be here at night.   139   **wot:** know
I'll to him, he is hid at Lawrence' cell.   140

Juliet   O find him! Give this ring to my true knight,
And bid him come to take his last farewell.   *Exit both.*

Romeo and Friar Lawrence, 2004.

Pick one of the following three lines, which you think Romeo is most likely to have been saying when this photo was taken. Give reasons for your answer.

a) But "banishèd" to kill me? "Banishèd"? (line 46)

b) It helps not, it prevails not. Talk no more. (line 60)

c) Mist-like, enfold me from the search of eyes. (line 74)

Tom Burke, John McEnery

ACT 3 SCENE 3

Enter Friar Lawrence.

Lawrence	Romeo, come forth, come forth thou fearful man.	
	Affliction is enamoured of thy parts,	
	And thou art wedded to calamity. *[Enter Romeo.]*	
Romeo	Father, what news? What is the Prince's doom?	
	What sorrow craves acquaintance at my hand	5
	That I yet know not?	
Friar Lawrence	Too familiar	
	Is my dear son with such sour company.	
	I bring thee tidings of the Prince's doom.	
Romeo	What less than doomsday is the Prince's doom?	
Friar Lawrence	A gentler judgement vanished from his lips,	10
	Not body's death, but body's banishment.	
Romeo	Ha, banishment? Be merciful, say "death".	
	For exile hath more terror in his look,	
	Much more than death. Do not say "banishment."	
Friar Lawrence	Hence from Verona art thou banishèd.	15
	Be patient, for the world is broad and wide.	

1 **fearful:** frightened
2 **Affliction is enamoured of thy parts:** misery is attracted to you
3 **calamity:** disaster
4 **doom:** judgement
5 **craves acquaintance at my hand:** is waiting to be introduced
6–7 **Too familiar Is my dear son ... company:** you are miserable enough as it is
8 **tidings:** news

9 **doomsday:** the Day of Judgement (death)
10 **vanished:** came

70

Romeo There is no world without Verona walls
But purgatory, torture, hell itself.
Hence "banishèd" is banished from the world,
And world's exile is death. Then banishèd   20
Is death mistermed. Calling death "banishèd,"
Thou cutt'st my head off with a golden axe
And smil'st upon the stroke that murders me.

Friar Lawrence O deadly sin, O rude unthankfulness!
Thy fault our law calls death, but the kind Prince,   25
Taking thy part, hath rushed aside the law,
And turned that black word "death" to "banishment."
This is dear mercy, and thou seest it not.

Romeo 'Tis torture, and not mercy. Heav'n is here
Where Juliet lives, and every cat and dog   30
And little mouse, every unworthy thing,
Live here in heaven and may look on her,
But Romeo may not. More validity,
More honourable state, more courtship lives
In carrion flies than Romeo. They may seize   35
On the white wonder of dear Juliet's hand
And steal immortal blessing from her lips,
Who even in pure and vestal modesty,
Still blush, as thinking their own kisses sin.
But Romeo may not, he is banishèd.   40
This may flies do, when I from this must fly.
They are free men, but I am banishèd.
And say'st thou yet that exile is not death?
Hadst thou no poison mixed, no sharp-ground knife,
No sudden mean of death, though ne'er so mean,   45
But "banishèd" to kill me? "Banishèd"?
O Friar, the damnèd use that word in hell.
Howlings attend it. How hast thou the heart,
Being a divine, a ghostly confessor,
A sin-absolver, and my friend professed,   50
To mangle me with that word "banishèd"?

Friar Lawrence Thou fond mad man, hear me a little speak.

Romeo O thou wilt speak again of banishment.

Friar Lawrence I'll give thee armour to keep off that word,
Adversity's sweet milk, philosophy,   55
To comfort thee, though thou art banishèd.

Romeo Yet "banishèd"? Hang up philosophy,
Unless philosophy can make a Juliet,
Displant a town, reverse a prince's doom,
It helps not, it prevails not. Talk no more.   60

Friar Lawrence O then I see that mad men have no ears.

Romeo How should they, when that wise men have no eyes?

Friar Lawrence Let me dispute with thee of thy estate.

Romeo Thou canst not speak of that thou dost not feel.
Wert thou as young as I, Juliet thy love,   65

17 **without Verona walls:** outside Verona
18 **But:** except
18 **purgatory:** where Catholics believe the souls of the dead suffered for sin before being allowed into Heaven
19 **Hence "banishèd":** to be banished from Verona
20 **world's exile:** to be exiled from the world
21 **mistermed:** under the wrong name
24 **O deadly sin, O rude unthankfulness!:** such ingratitude in wishing for death will damn your soul to Hell
25 **Thy fault our law calls death:** the punishment for your crime is death
26 **rushed:** forced
28 **dear:** a valuable
33 **validity:** value
34 **honourable state:** respect
34 **courtship:** double meaning: the chance to woo; gentlemanly behaviour
34–5 **lives In carrion-flies:** is possible for flies that live on rotting flesh
38 **vestal:** virginal
43 **say'st thou yet:** do you still say
44 **Hadst thou no:** haven't you any
45 **No sudden mean of death:** any quick way to kill myself
45 **though ne'er so mean:** no matter how unpleasant
48 **Howlings attend it:** they howl as they do so
49 **divine:** churchman
49 **ghostly:** spiritual
50 **my friend professed:** someone who says he's my friend
51 **mangle me:** mutilate me
52 **fond:** foolish

55 **Adversity's sweet milk, philosophy:** the best addition to trouble: the ability to think through the problem and accept it
57 **Yet:** still
57 **Hang up:** put away
59 **Displant:** move
60 **it prevails not:** it doesn't convince me

62 **when that:** when

63 **Let me dispute with thee of thy estate:** let's discuss your situation

71

ACT 3 SCENE 3

An hour but married, Tybalt murderèd,
Doting like me and like me banishèd.
Then mightst thou speak.
Then mightst thou tear thy hair,
And fall upon the ground, as I do now,   70
Taking the measure of an unmade grave.

Knocking within.

Friar Lawrence Arise, one knocks, good Romeo, hide thyself.

Romeo Not I, unless the breath of heartsick groans,
Mist-like, enfold me from the search of eyes. *Knocking.*

Friar Lawrence Hark, how they knock! — Who's there?— Romeo, arise!   75
Thou wilt be taken. — Stay awhile! — Stand up.

Knocking.

Run to my study. — By and by! — God's will,
What simpleness is this? — I come, I come! *Knocking.*
Who knocks so hard?
Whence come you? What's your will?   80

66 **An hour but married:** only married an hour ago
67 **Doting:** deeply in love

71 **Taking the measure of:** measuring out

72 **one:** someone
73–4 **the breath of heartsick groans … search of eyes:** my groaning makes a mist that hides me from sight
76 **taken:** arrested
76 **Stay awhile!:** wait a minute (to the person knocking)
77 **By and by!:** I'm on my way (to the person knocking)
78 **simpleness:** stupidity
80 **What's your will?:** what do you want?

Romeo and the Nurse, 2013.

All these photos were taken after the Nurse enters. In what order were they taken? Support your choice with reference to the text.

Will Featherstone, Lisa Stevenson

Nurse	*[Within.]* Let me come in, and you shall know my errand.	
	I come from Lady Juliet.	
Friar Lawrence	Welcome then. *Enter Nurse.*	
Nurse	O holy Friar, O tell me holy Friar,	
	Where is my lady's lord? Where's Romeo?	85
Friar Lawrence	There on the ground, with his own tears made drunk.	
Nurse	O, he is even in my mistress' case,	
	Just in her case. O woeful sympathy!	
	Piteous predicament! Even so lies she,	
	Blubbering and weeping, weeping and blubbering.	90
	Stand up, stand up, stand and you be a man:	
	For Juliet's sake, for her sake, rise and stand.	
	Why should you fall into so deep an O?	
Romeo	Nurse.	
Nurse	Ah sir, ah sir, death's the end of all.	
Romeo	Speak'st thou of Juliet? How is it with her?	95
	Doth she not think me an old murderer,	
	Now I have stained the childhood of our joy	
	With blood removed but little from her own?	
	Where is she? And how doth she? And what says	
	My concealed lady to our cancelled love?	100
Nurse	O, she says nothing, sir, but weeps and weeps,	
	And now falls on her bed, and then starts up,	
	And Tybalt calls, and then on Romeo cries,	
	And then down falls again.	
Romeo	As if that name,	
	Shot from the deadly level of a gun,	105
	Did murder her; as that name's cursed hand	
	Murdered her kinsman. O tell me, Friar, tell me,	
	In what vile part of this anatomy	
	Doth my name lodge? Tell me, that I may sack	
	The hateful mansion. *[Drawing his dagger.]*	
Friar Lawrence	Hold thy desperate hand.	110
	Art thou a man? Thy form cries out thou art.	
	Thy tears are womanish, thy wild acts denote	
	The unreasonable fury of a beast.	
	Unseemly woman in a seeming man,	
	And ill-beseeming beast in seeming both,	115
	Thou hast amazed me. By my holy order,	
	I thought thy disposition better tempered.	
	Hast thou slain Tybalt? Wilt thou slay thyself?	
	And slay thy lady that in thy life lies,	
	By doing damnèd hate upon thyself?	120
	Why rail'st thou on thy birth, the heav'n and earth?	
	Since birth, and heav'n, and earth, all three do meet	
	In thee at once, which thou at once wouldst lose.	
	Fie, fie, thou sham'st thy shape, thy love, thy wit,	
	Which like a usurer abound'st in all.	125
	And usest none in that true use indeed	

87 even in my mistress' case: in the same state as my mistress
88 woeful sympathy: how alike in misery
89 Piteous predicament: you pity their situation
91 and you be: if you are
93 so deep an O: such wailing
96 old: clever, skilful
97 the childhood of our joy: our newly-made relationship
98 removed ... her own: of a close relative
100 My concealed lady: my secret wife
100 cancelled: ended, removed
103 on Romeo cries: calls out for Romeo
104 that name: Romeo
105 level: aim
108 this anatomy: my body
109 lodge: live
109–10 sack ... mansion: destroy its home
111 Thy form cries out thou art: you look like one
112 denote: show
113 unreasonable: not thought through
114–5 Unseemly woman ... seeming both: your womanish behaviour isn't right for the man you appear to be; your animal behaviour suits neither man nor woman
117 disposition: character, nature
119 thy lady that in thy life lies: your wife whose life depends on yours
120 doing damnèd hate upon thyself: committing suicide (which Catholics at the time believed damned you to Hell)
121 rail'st thou on: do you abuse
121 heav'n and earth: your soul and body
123 at once wouldst lose: now want to destroy
124 thy shape: your body
124 thy wit: your intelligence
125–7 like a usurer ... thy wit: like a money-lender with money, you have so much of and aren't using properly

SHAKESPEARE'S WORLD

Clandestine marriage

Romeo and Juliet's marriage ceremony was *clandestine* because they married secretly, and without going through the proper procedures. Since they were both under twenty-one, they needed their parents' consent to marry. Romeo, Juliet and Friar Lawrence all put themselves at risk by this secret marriage. All of them had broken the law. Courts wanted to make sure that all marriages were legal, so they punished priests who performed weddings under irregular circumstances. Other people, including the parents, could challenge a marriage that they did not think was lawful, and have it declared void. All three could be forced to pay a fine or serve public penance for their actions.

Here, Friar Lawrence encourages Romeo to go to Juliet before he leaves Verona for exile. This gives them an opportunity to consummate their marriage. Once a marriage was consummated, the courts were much less likely to declare it void. By encouraging Romeo to consummate his marriage, Friar Lawrence tries to prevent the courts from acting against it.

Actor's view

Colin Hurley
Friar Lawrence, spring 2009

So, what's actually happened is he's killed someone and he is in hiding at my place. I've gone out to find out what the word on the street is, come back, call him out:

'come forth, come forth, thou fearful man.'

And then I tell him that there's good news and there's bad news. Strictly speaking, he should be killed of course, because that's what the Prince said but he says 'No, no, you're going to be banished' so, that's a good thing. Romeo, being a young man in love and a bit on the melodramatic side, goes on about it being torture not mercy. I have to talk him out of his despair, with a lot of talk of his unthankfulness being a sin. I mean we kind of had a bit of a spat. I love that:

'[Friar] O then I see that mad men have no ears.

[Romeo] How should they, when that wise men have no eyes?

[Friar] Let me dispute with thee of thy estate.

[Romeo] Thou canst not speak of that thou dost not feel.'

and I found that very interesting. That this young guy goes 'What do you know about where I am emotionally? How would you know? You're an old bloke, you're fiddling about with your flowers and your herbs, you're a virgin, and you try to tell me' and so he is. I find that with youth now, they can say 'You don't understand, there's no way you understand.' And it's sort of true and it sort of isn't.

exam SKILLS

Target skill: analysis of a character's language and role

Question: How does Shakespeare present the Friar in this speech?

Shakespeare often uses friars in his plays as people who suggest plans. Here the Friar tries to take on the role of *deus ex machina* (a power that comes in the nick of time to solve a difficulty). He is a plot vehicle whose role here furthers the action of the play and helps us to understand Romeo's character. Read the Shakespeare's World section on secret marriage, to help you appreciate the significance of consummating an illegal marriage, and to understand why the Friar helps Romeo to spend the night with Juliet.

1 With a partner:
- Count the questions in lines 110–120.
- Count how many times the Friar uses triple references (groups of three) as in "thy shape, thy love, thy wit".
- Identify the similes ("Like powder…").
- Find the repetition in lines 135–145.

How does Shakespeare use these techniques to encourage Romeo to listen to the speech?

2 The tone of the Friar's speech changes at line 148 ("Go get thee to thy love…"). *What do you notice about the verbs in this section of the speech? Find all the Friar's imperatives (instructions) telling Romeo how to act. How do they influence the mood of the scene?*

3 How far do you agree with the statements below? Decide which you agree with most and least.

a) The Friar's diatribe is so insulting that the audience will find it hard to think Romeo deserves to survive and thrive.

b) The Friar succeeds in diverting Romeo's thoughts of suicide and makes him act positively.

c) The Friar's speech is useful in plot terms because it informs the audience while advising Romeo.

4 How do the insights you have gained help you answer the question above?

Which should bedeck thy shape, thy love, thy wit.
Thy noble shape is but a form of wax,
Digressing from the valour of a man,
Thy dear love sworn but hollow perjury,   130
Killing that love which thou hast vowed to cherish.
Thy wit, that ornament to shape and love,
Misshapen in the conduct of them both, ·
Like powder in a skilless soldier's flask,
Is set afire by thine own ignorance,   135
And thou dismembered with thine own defence.
What, rouse thee man, thy Juliet is alive,
For whose dear sake thou wast but lately dead.
There art thou happy. Tybalt would kill thee,
But thou slew'st Tybalt. There art thou happy   140
The law that threatened death becomes thy friend
And turns it to exile. There art thou happy.
A pack of blessings light upon thy back,
Happiness courts thee in her best array,
But like a mishavèd and sullen wench,   145
Thou pouts upon thy fortune and thy love.
Take heed, take heed, for such die miserable.
Go get thee to thy love as was decreed,
Ascend her chamber, hence and comfort her.
But look thou stay not till the watch be set,   150
For then thou canst not pass to Mantua,
Where thou shalt live, till we can find a time
To blaze your marriage, reconcile your friends,
Beg pardon of the Prince, and call thee back
With twenty hundred thousand times more joy   155
Than thou went'st forth in lamentation.
Go before nurse, commend me to thy lady,
And bid her hasten all the house to bed,
Which heavy sorrow makes them apt unto.
Romeo is coming.   160

Nurse   O Lord, I could have stayed here all the night
To hear good counsel. O what learning is!
— My lord, I'll tell my lady you will come.

Romeo   Do so, and bid my sweet prepare to chide.

Nurse   Here sir, a ring she bid me give you sir.   165
Hie you, make haste, for it grows very late.   *Exit Nurse.*

Romeo   How well my comfort is revived by this,

Friar Lawrence   Go hence, good night, and here stands all your state:
Either be gone before the watch be set,
Or by the break of day disguised from hence.   170
Sojourn in Mantua, I'll find out your man,
And he shall signify from time to time
Every good hap to you that chances here.
Give me thy hand, 'tis late. Farewell, good night.

Romeo   But that a joy past joy calls out on me,   175
It were a grief so brief to part with thee.
Farewell.   *They exit.*

128-9 **form of wax ... of a man:** not a living, thinking man capable of bravery
130 **Thy dear love ... perjury:** the love you have sworn is nothing but lies
133 **Misshapen ... them both:** is thinking wrongly about killing both of them
136 **dismembered with thine own defence:** blown apart by the thing meant to protect you
138 **but lately dead:** trying to kill yourself over
139 **happy:** fortunate
143 **light:** land
144 **array:** clothes and jewels
145 **mishavèd:** badly behaved
145 **sullen wench:** sulky girl
147 **such:** people like that
148 **as was decreed:** as you planned
150 **look:** make sure that
150 **till the watch be set:** until the watchmen go on guard at night
151 **pass:** go out of the city gates
153 **blaze:** tell everyone about
153 **reconcile your friends:** get your families to accept it
156 **lamentation:** sorrow
157 **before:** ahead
159 **apt unto:** likely to do
164 **chide:** tell me off
168 **here stands all your state:** your future depends on this
171 **Sojourn:** stay for a while
172 **signify:** bring you news
173 **good hap to you that chances here:** everything that's happening in Verona
175 **calls out on me:** calls me away
176 **It were a grief ... part with thee:** I'd be sorry to leave you in such a hurry

---

Director's Note, 3.3

✔ Friar Lawrence tells Romeo his punishment is banishment, not death.

✔ Romeo insists banishment from Juliet is worse than death. He falls to the ground, weeping.

✔ The Nurse arrives, saying Juliet is in a similar state.

✔ Romeo fears Juliet must hate him for killing Tybalt, and tries to stab himself, but is stopped by the Friar (and, perhaps, the Nurse).

✔ The Friar sends Romeo to spend the night with Juliet, telling him he must go to Mantua before daybreak.

✔ Does Shakespeare show Romeo acting like a teenager in love?

Enter Capulet, Lady Capulet, and Paris.

Capulet	Things have fallen out, sir, so unluckily,	1 **fallen out:** turned out
	That we have had no time to move our daughter.	2 **to move:** to persuade
	Look you, she loved her kinsman Tybalt dearly,	
	And so did I. Well, we were born to die.	
	'Tis very late, she'll not come down to-night. 5	
	I promise you, but for your company,	
	I would have been a-bed an hour ago.	
Paris	These times of woe afford no time to woo.	8 **afford:** give
	Madam, good night, commend me to your daughter.	
Lady Capulet	I will, and know her mind early tomorrow, 10	10 **know her mind:** I'll make her decide
	To-night she is mewed up to her heaviness.	11 **mewed up to her heaviness:** shut up in her misery
Capulet	Sir Paris, I will make a desperate tender	12 **desperate tender:** bold offer
	Of my child's love. I think she will be ruled	
	In all respects by me. Nay, more, I doubt it not.	
	Wife, go you to her ere you go to bed, 15	15 **ere:** before
	Acquaint her here of my son Paris' love,	16 **son:** Capulet has accepted the marriage, so already treats Paris as his son-in-law
	And bid her, mark you me, on Wednesday next —	17 **bid her:** tell her
	But soft, what day is this?	17 **mark you me:** listen carefully now
		18 **soft:** wait a minute
Paris	Monday, my lord.	
Capulet	Monday! Ha, Ha! Well, Wednesday is too soon, 20	
	O' Thursday let it be. O' Thursday, tell her,	
	She shall be married to this noble earl.	
	Will you be ready? Do you like this haste?	
	We'll keep no great ado, a friend or two,	24 **We'll keep no great ado:** we won't have a big fussy wedding
	For hark you, Tybalt being slain so late, 25	25 **hark you:** listen
	It may be thought we held him carelessly,	25 **so late:** so recently
	Being our kinsman, if we revel much.	26–7 **held him carelessly … revel much:** a big celebration may look as if we didn't care about his death, even though he's family
	Therefore we'll have some half a dozen friends,	
	And there an end. But what say you to Thursday?	29 **And there an end:** no more
		30 **I would:** I wish
Paris	My lord, I would that Thursday were tomorrow. 30	
Capulet	Well, get you gone, o' Thursday be it, then.	
	— Go you to Juliet ere you go to bed,	33 **against:** for
	Prepare her wife, against this wedding day.	35 **Afore me:** double meaning: an exclamation (e.g. well, well); an instruction to the servant to go in front with the light
	— Farewell, my lord. — Light to my chamber, ho!	
	Afore me, it is so very late, that we 35	
	May call it early by and by. Good night. *They exit.*	36 **by and by:** soon

Director's Note, 3.4

✔ Capulet suddenly changes his mind, and tells Paris he can marry Juliet in three days' time.

✔ Capulet says it will be a quiet wedding because of the death of Tybalt.

✔ He tells his wife to prepare Juliet.

✔ How has Capulet changed since Act 1 Scene 2?

ACT 3 SCENE 5

Enter Romeo and Juliet aloft.

Juliet   Wilt thou be gone? It is not yet near day.
It was the nightingale, and not the lark,
That pierced the fearful hollow of thine ear,
Nightly she sings on yon pomegranate tree.
Believe me, love, it was the nightingale.   5

Romeo   It was the lark, the herald of the morn,
No nightingale. Look, love, what envious streaks
Do lace the severing clouds in yonder east.
Night's candles are burnt out, and jocund day
Stands tiptoe on the misty mountain tops.   10
I must be gone and live, or stay and die.

Juliet   Yond light is not daylight, I know it, I.
It is some meteor that the sun exhales
To be to thee this night a torch-bearer
And light thee on thy way to Mantua.   15
Therefore stay yet, thou need'st not to be gone.

Romeo   Let me be ta'en, let me be put to death,
I am content, so thou wilt have it so.
I'll say yon grey is not the morning's eye,
'Tis but the pale reflex of Cynthia's brow.   20
Nor that is not the lark whose notes do beat
The vaulty heaven so high above our heads.
I have more care to stay than will to go.
Come death and welcome, Juliet wills it so.
How is't, my soul? Let's talk, it is not day.   25

Juliet   It is, it is, hie hence, be gone, away.
It is the lark that sings so out of tune,
Straining harsh discords and unpleasing sharps.
Some say the lark makes sweet division.
This doth not so, for she divideth us.   30
Some say the lark and loathèd toad change eyes,
O now I would they had changed voices too,
Since arm from arm that voice doth us affray,
Hunting thee hence with hunt's-up to the day.
O now be gone, more light and light it grows.   35

Romeo   More light and light, more dark and dark our woes!

Enter Nurse.

Nurse   Madam!

Juliet   Nurse?

Nurse   Your lady mother is coming to your chamber.
The day is broke, be wary, look about.   *[She exits.]* 40

Juliet   Then window let day in, and let life out.

Romeo   Farewell, farewell. One kiss and I'll descend.

He climbs down.

Juliet   Art thou gone so? Love, lord, ay husband, friend,

2 **nightingale/lark:** nightingales sing in the evening, larks sing at dawn
3 **fearful:** frightened
7–8 **what envious streaks ... yonder east:** dawn is coming, making the clouds pink, envious of our love
9 **Night's candles:** the stars
9 **jocund:** cheerful
13 **exhales:** breathes out
17 **ta'en:** taken, arrested
18 **so thou wilt have it so:** if that is what you want
20 **reflex of Cynthia's brow:** the reflection of the moon goddess's face (Cynthia was another name for Diana, moon goddess)
21 **Nor that is not:** and that is not
22 **vaulty:** dome-like
23 **care:** desire
26 **hie hence:** hurry away from here
28 **sharps:** sharp musical notes
29 **sweet division:** a quick run of musical notes
30 **This doth not so:** I don't think so
31 **change:** exchange (from a folk tale told to explain why toads have more beautiful eyes than larks)
33 **arm from arm ... affray:** the lark's voice sends us from each other's arms in fear
34 **hunt's-up:** a song to wake hunters
40 **wary:** cautious

77

I must hear from thee every day in the hour,
For in a minute there are many days.   45
O by this count I shall be much in years
Ere I again behold my Romeo!

Romeo   Farewell.
                    I will omit no opportunity
                    That may convey my greetings, love, to thee.   50

Juliet   O think'st thou we shall ever meet again?

Romeo   I doubt it not, and all these woes shall serve
                    For sweet discourses in our time to come.

Juliet   O God! I have an ill-divining soul.
                    Methinks I see thee now, thou art so low,   55
                    As one dead in the bottom of a tomb.
                    Either my eyesight fails, or thou look'st pale.

Romeo   And trust me love, in my eye so do you.
                    Dry sorrow drinks our blood. Adieu, adieu.   *Exit.*

46 **count:** way of adding up
46 **much in years:** very old

50 **convey:** bring
52–3 **all these woes ... time to come:** we'll talk about these sorrows in the future
54 **I have an ill-divining soul:** I feel in my soul that bad things are going to happen

55 **so low:** so far down (the ladder)

59 **Dry:** thirsty

FROM THE REHEARSAL ROOM...

WHAT I SAY, WHAT I HEAR AND WHAT I THINK

- Work in groups of four: A, B, C and D.
- Each group should work on one of these sections: lines 64–74; 74–84; 84–95; 93–104, 103–117; 116–125
- Read through your lines. A is Juliet, B is Lady Capulet and C and D are noting down when Juliet is deceiving her mother by saying something which she means in one way, but which her mother understands differently.
- On separate A4 sheets, write in large letters short phrases or words that show what Juliet might be thinking each time there is a major difference between what she says and what she thinks.
- On separate A4 sheets, write in large letters short phrases or words that show what Lady Capulet assumes each time there is a major difference between what Juliet says and what she thinks.
- Re-read the extract; this time C is Juliet's inner thoughts and D is Lady Capulet's interpretation of what Juliet says. Whenever there is a gap between what Juliet says to her mother and what she is thinking to herself, C holds up a sheet with Juliet's inner thoughts and D holds up a sheet with what Lady Capulet thinks she hears.
- Share your sections, so the class sees the whole dialogue. *What different interpretations were there of the repeated lines?*

1 What does Shakespeare show the audience about the relationship between Juliet and her mother in this extract?

2 How do you think this extract works on stage?

SHAKESPEARE'S WORLD

Asides

Asides are common in Shakespeare's plays. When a character speaks, and some or all of the characters on stage can't hear, it is an aside. In this scene, when Juliet is talking to herself and her mother cannot hear, it is an aside. She is sharing her thoughts with the audience. This is an important part of Shakespeare's craft as a playwright. When a character speaks alone onstage, we call it a soliloquy. Shakespeare uses asides and soliloquies to tell us what a character is really thinking. When Romeo sees Juliet on the balcony, he asks the audience if he should speak to her. Here Juliet tells us how much she loves Romeo, even while Lady Capulet is plotting to kill him. In the original playhouse, as in today's Globe, nobody in the audience was very far from the stage. This means that asides and soliloquies are intimate moments, shared between the character and the audience.

Juliet	O Fortune, Fortune, all men call thee fickle.	60

Juliet   O Fortune, Fortune, all men call thee fickle.   60
If thou art fickle, what dost thou with him
That is renowned for faith? Be fickle, Fortune,
For then I hope thou wilt not keep him long,
But send him back.   *Enter Lady Capulet.*

Lady Capulet   Ho daughter, are you up?

Juliet   Who is't that calls? It is my lady mother.   65
Is she not down so late, or up so early?
What unaccustomed cause procures her hither?

Lady Capulet   Why how now, Juliet?

Juliet   Madam, I am not well.

Lady Capulet   Evermore weeping for your cousin's death?
What, wilt thou wash him from his grave with tears?   70
An if thou couldst, thou couldst not make him live.
Therefore have done. Some grief shows much of love,
But much of grief, shows still some want of wit.

Juliet   Yet let me weep, for such a feeling loss.

Lady Capulet   So shall you feel the loss, but not the friend   75
Which you weep for.

Juliet   Feeling so the loss,
Cannot choose but ever weep the friend.

Lady Capulet   Well, girl, thou weep'st not so much for his death,
As that the villain lives which slaughtered him.

Juliet   What villain, madam?

Lady Capulet   That same villain, Romeo.   80

Juliet   *[Aside.]*   Villain and he be many miles asunder. —
God pardon him! I do, with all my heart,
And yet no man like he doth grieve my heart.

Lady Capulet   That is because the traitor murderer lives.

Juliet   Ay, madam, from the reach of these my hands.   85
Would none but I might venge my cousin's death.

Lady Capulet   We will have vengeance for it, fear thou not.
Then weep no more, I'll send to one in Mantua,
Where that same banished runagate doth live,
Shall give him such an unaccustomed dram,   90
That he shall soon keep Tybalt company.
And then I hope thou wilt be satisfied.

Juliet   *[Aside.]*   Indeed I never shall be satisfied
With Romeo till I behold him, dead
Is my poor heart so, for a kinsman vex'd?   95
Madam, if you could find out but a man
To bear a poison, I would temper it,
That Romeo should, upon receipt thereof,
Soon sleep in quiet. O, how my heart abhors
To hear him named, and cannot come to him.   100
To wreak the love I bore my cousin
Upon his body that slaughtered him.

60 **fickle:** changeable
61 **what dost thou:** what do you want from
62 **renowned for faith:** known to be faithful

66 **Is she not down … up so early:** I wonder if she's up early or hasn't been to bed
67 **procures her hither:** brings her here
68 **how now:** what's wrong

72 **have done:** stop weeping
73 **shows stills some want of wit:** is always foolish
74 **feeling:** deeply felt

77 **friend:** can also mean 'lover'; Juliet's mother talks of Tybalt, Juliet of Romeo. From this point, she is deliberately misleading her mother over her feelings for Romeo

81 **Villain and he … miles asunder:** Romeo is far from being a villain
83 **no man like he doth grieve my heart:** no man can cause me the distress he has

86 **Would:** I wish
86 **venge:** take revenge for

89 **runagate:** runaway
90 **unaccustomed dram:** unusual drink (of poison)

95 **vex'd:** made angry

97 **temper:** mix something into
98 **upon receipt thereof:** when he has it
99 **abhors:** hates
101 **wreak:** 'work' double meaning: have her revenge; show her love

At this point (line 143), do you think Shakespeare intended the actor to play Capulet as genuinely angry, or just tactically angry to get Juliet to do what he wants? Support your answer with reference to the text.

Jade Anouka, Jason Baughan

exam SKILLS

Target skill: understanding relationships

Question: Look at how Juliet and her mother speak and behave here. What does it reveal to an audience about their relationship at this point in the play? Refer closely to details from the extract to support your answer.

As the example above shows, the exam extract question may ask you to look at relationships at a particular point of the play. In questions of this kind, you:

- may use your knowledge of the characters' behaviour in other parts of the play, but concentrate on the given extract. Note that the question reads "at this point in the play".
- should put the extract in place, saying what has happened just before. You don't have to give the act and scene.
- should use a **P**oint-**E**vidence-**E**xplanation structure.
- should include a spread of points from across the extract.
- should pay close attention to language and techniques. Note that the question reads "refer closely to details". For example: Lady Capulet uses triple adjectives to stress Paris' qualities; Juliet repeats her mother's words to mock them; Juliet repeats the pronoun "I" to show the strength of her feelings.

SHAKESPEARE'S WORLD

Family life

In this scene, Capulet is angry because Juliet disobeys him by saying she will not marry Paris. Shakespeare's audience lived in a world where the father or husband was the head of the household, and in charge of the family. The Church taught that children should obey their parents, and wives should submit to their husbands. This reflected a male-dominated society – only men could vote, go to university, or be a doctor or lawyer. Both Lady Capulet and Juliet were expected to obey Capulet in everything. Since Juliet is a girl, her boldness is even more troubling to her father – she is breaking two obligations, to obey as a child, and as a female. Many parents were strict with their children to teach them discipline and respect. People thought spoiling children was wrong, because the children would become rude and selfish. While this might seem harsh today, parents usually acted in their child's best interest. In the play, Capulet wants Juliet to marry Paris since he will be able to provide for her later in life. In Shakespeare's day, children's actions also showed others their social class. Juliet's disrespectfulness towards her father would be an insult to the training he had provided for her as a child. Parents expected their children to be obedient and show their high social status to their neighbours.

Lady Capulet	Find thou the means, and I'll find such a man.
	But now I'll tell thee joyful tidings, girl.
Juliet	And joy comes well in such a needy time,
	What are they, I beseech your ladyship?
Lady Capulet	Well, well, thou hast a careful father, child!
	One who to put thee from thy heaviness
	Hath sorted out a sudden day of joy,
	That thou expect'st not, nor I looked not for.
Juliet	Madam, in happy time, what day is that?
Lady Capulet	Marry my child, early next Thursday morn,
	The gallant, young and noble gentleman,
	The County Paris, at Saint Peter's Church,
	Shall happily make thee there a joyful bride.
Juliet	Now, by Saint Peter's Church, and Peter too,
	He shall not make me there a joyful bride.
	I wonder at this haste, that I must wed
	Ere he that should be husband comes to woo.
	I pray you, tell my lord and father, madam,
	I will not marry yet, and when I do, I swear
	It shall be Romeo, whom you know I hate,
	Rather than Paris. These are news indeed!
Lady Capulet	Here comes your father, tell him so yourself,
	And see how he will take it at your hands.

Enter Capulet and Nurse.

Capulet	When the sun sets, the air doth drizzle dew,
	But for the sunset of my brother's son
	It rains downright. —
	How now? A conduit, girl? What, still in tears?
	Evermore show'ring? In one little body
	Thou counterfeits a bark, a sea, a wind.
	For still thy eyes, which I may call the sea,
	Do ebb and flow with tears. The bark thy body is,
	Sailing in this salt flood, the winds thy sighs,
	Who, raging with thy tears and they with them,
	Without a sudden calm will overset
	Thy tempest-tossed body. How now, wife?
	Have you delivered to her our decree?
Lady Capulet	Ay, sir, but she will none, she gives you thanks.
	I would the fool were married to her grave.
Capulet	Soft, take me with you, take me with you, wife.
	How, will she none? Doth she not give us thanks?
	Is she not proud? Doth she not count her blest,
	Unworthy as she is, that we have wrought
	So worthy a gentleman to be her bridegroom?
Juliet	Not proud you have, but thankful, that you have.
	Proud can I never be of what I hate,
	But thankful even for hate, that is meant love.
Capulet	How, how, how, how? Chopped-logic? What is this?
	"Proud", and "I thank you", and "I thank you not".

105

110

115

120

125

130

135

140

145

150

---

105 **in such a needy time:** at a time when we need it most

107 **careful:** caring
108 **heaviness:** sadness
109 **sorted out:** arranged
110 **nor I looked not for:** and I wasn't expecting
111 **in happy time:** how lucky

112 **Marry:** a mild oath – by Mary (Christ's mother)

118 **I wonder at:** I'm astonished at
119 **Ere he that ... comes to woo:** before the man who wants to be my husband has even begun to court me

123 **These are news indeed!:** what a thing to tell me

125 **at your hands:** from you

127 **the sunset of my brother's son:** Tybalt's death
129 **conduit:** water pipe

131 **Thou counterfeits:** you imitate
131 **bark:** ship
132 **still:** always

136 **Without:** unless there is

138 **our decree:** my decision

139 **she will none:** she won't do it

141 **Soft, take me with you:** hold on, explain
143 **count her:** consider herself
144 **wrought:** persuaded
146 **Not proud you have, but thankful:** I'm not pleased, but I am grateful
148 **thankful even for hate, that is meant love:** I'm grateful for what you have done out of love, but I hate the thing itself
149 **Chopped-logic:** over-clever arguments

Lady Capulet, Juliet (kneeling), Capulet, summer 2009.

1 What is the earliest point in the scene this photo might have been taken? Quote from the text to support your answer.
2 How has the director chosen to make Juliet look at this point in the scene? Explain your answer.

l–r Miranda Foster, Ellie Kendrick, Ian Redford

And yet "not proud", mistress minion you?
Thank me no thankings, nor, proud me no prouds,
But fettle your fine joints 'gainst Thursday next,
To go with Paris to Saint Peter's Church,
Or I will drag thee on a hurdle thither.
Out you green-sickness carrion, out you baggage,
You tallow-face!

Lady Capulet   Fie, fie, what, are you mad?

Juliet   Good father, I beseech you on my knees,
Hear me with patience but to speak a word.

Capulet   Hang thee young baggage, disobedient wretch!
I tell thee what, get thee to church o' Thursday,
Or never after look me in the face.
Speak not, reply not, do not answer me.
My fingers itch. Wife, we scarce thought us blest
That God had lent us but this only child,
But now I see this one is one too much,
And that we have a curse in having her.
Out on her, hilding!

Nurse   God in heav'n bless her!
You are to blame, my lord, to rate her so.

Capulet   And why, my lady wisdom? hold your tongue,
Good prudence, smatter with your gossips, go.

Nurse   I speak no treason.

Capulet   O, God gi' good-e'en.

Nurse   May not one speak?

Capulet   Peace, you mumbling fool!
Utter your gravity o'er a gossip's bowl,
For here we need it not.

Lady Capulet   You are too hot.

Capulet   God's bread, it makes me mad!
Day, night, hour, tide, time, work, play,
Alone, in company, still my care hath been
To have her matched. And having now provided
A gentleman of noble parentage,
Of fair demesnes, youthful, and nobly allied,
Stuffed, as they say, with honourable parts,
Proportioned as one's thought would wish a man —
And then to have a wretched puling fool,
A whining mammet, in her fortune's tender,
To answer, "I'll not wed, I cannot love.
I am too young, I pray you, pardon me."
But, and you will not wed, I'll pardon you!
Graze where you will you shall not house with me.
Look to't, think on't, I do not use to jest.
Thursday is near, lay hand on heart, advise.
An you be mine, I'll give you to my friend.
And you be not: hang, beg, starve, die in the streets,
For, by my soul, I'll ne'er acknowledge thee,

151 mistress minion: spoilt little madam
153 fettle your fine joints: get your fussy self ready
155 **155 hurdle:** rough wooden frame used to drag traitors to execution
156 Out: used to show disgust
156 green-sickness carrion: bloodless corpse
156 baggage: a good-for nothing woman
157 tallow-face: face as white as candle wax
160 **157 fie:** used to reproach someone for unsuitable behaviour

164 My fingers itch: I long to slap you
165 **165 but this only:** just one

168 hilding: a good-for nothing horse or woman
169 rate her so: scold her so violently
170
171 smatter with your gossips: babble away with your women friends
172 God gi' good-e'en: said to show he's exasperated

174 Utter your gravity o'er a gossip's bowl: say your piece when drinking with your friends
175

178-9 still my care hath been To have her matched: I've been constantly thinking about finding her a good husband
180 **181 fair demesnes:** with plenty of land and income
181 nobly allied: with important connections
184 puling: whining
185 **185 mammet:** doll
185 in her fortune's tender: when offered this good fortune
188 and: if
189 Graze where you will ... with me: you can fend for yourself, I won't have you in the house
190 **190 I do not use to jest:** I'm not joking
191 advise: think it over carefully
194 acknowledge thee: accept you as mine

Text focus: Act 3 Scene 5 lines 140–195

The exam essay question like the one below may be a thematic one. You can choose a selection of characters and events that help to present the theme. Look at how characters speak and behave **(AO1)**. Consider the language and technical effects that Shakespeare uses **(AO2)**. Remember that 5 of the marks are allocated for your vocabulary, sentence structures and spelling **(AO4)**.

An analysis of the end of Act 3 Scene 5 would not make up the whole of an essay on youth and age, but this would be a productive section to look at in this essay. The scene that started with the intimacy of the newly-weds, ends with Juliet an isolated, childlike figure, berated by her father. Her parents and even her Nurse turn against her. Here, older characters seem against younger. Youth and age do not understand each other.

(AO1) Response to characters and events:

- This is not the first time we have seen Capulet in a rage. *What provokes him this time? How is this similar to his anger with Tybalt?*

- How do you react to Juliet's behaviour? *Explain whether you think all audience members would react in the same way.*

(AO2) Language, structure and form:

- Capulet fires questions at his wife and daughter. *Why do you think he asks so many questions?*
- Find examples of Capulet's use of:
  a) alliteration
  b) violent language
  c) cruel imperatives
  d) blunt, monosyllabic words.
  What do they show us about Capulet's feelings?

(AO4) Vocabulary, sentence structure and spelling:

- Re-read this advice and note down any useful words that you can use in this essay.

Question: How does Shakespeare present relationships between parents and children in *Romeo and Juliet*? (25 marks)

Plan a response to this essay. Make sure you look back through the play and note other scenes that deal with the relationships between parents and children.

FROM THE REHEARSAL ROOM...

EXPECTATIONS THEN AND NOW

1 Read from line 199 to the end of the scene, and pick out all the places where modern life is different. Discuss the differences between family life now and what you know of family life in Shakespeare's time.

2 In modern society, what role could the Nurse have with the Capulet family?

3 What status would Juliet have had in an Elizabethan family? How does it compare with a modern family?

4 As a group, create two versions of this section of the scene, one Elizabethan, one modern. In each, show how the conventions of family life affect what happens.

   a) Compare both versions and discuss the similarities and differences in the interpretations with the rest of the class.

   b) Which version had the most impact?

   c) What words had the most effect in both versions of the scene?

Director's view

Dominic Dromgoole
Director, summer 2009

Her father is horrendous, her mother lets her down, the Nurse eventually lets her down as well, and she was a small bird, Ellie [Kendrick, who played Juliet], with a wonderful innocence and a wonderful fragility. That is what I really wanted to do. Just see how much authority someone delicate and small could have.

Director's Note, 3.5

✔ After spending the night together, Romeo and Juliet part. He goes off to exile in Mantua.

✔ Juliet's mother arrives. She tells Juliet of the plan to marry her to Paris in three days.

✔ Juliet refuses – when her father arrives, she refuses again. He loses his temper, telling Juliet she must marry Paris or he will throw her out of his house.

✔ Her parents leave. Juliet asks the Nurse for her advice, which is that Juliet should marry Paris.

✔ Juliet says nothing, but privately rejects the Nurse and goes to ask for Friar Lawrence's help.

✔ How do Juliet's emotions change during this scene?

	Nor what is mine shall never do thee good.	195
	Trust to't, bethink you, I'll not be forsworn.	*Exit.*
Juliet	Is there no pity sitting in the clouds,	
	That sees into the bottom of my grief?	
	O sweet my mother, cast me not away.	
	Delay this marriage for a month, a week,	200
	Or, if you do not, make the bridal bed	
	In that dim monument where Tybalt lies.	
Lady Capulet	Talk not to me, for I'll not speak a word.	
	Do as thou wilt, for I have done with thee.	*Exit.*
Juliet	O God! O Nurse, how shall this be prevented?	205
	My husband is on earth, my faith in heaven,	
	How shall that faith return again to earth	
	Unless that husband send it me from heaven	
	By leaving earth? Comfort me, counsel me.	
	Alack, alack, that heaven should practise stratagems	210
	Upon so soft a subject as myself.	
	What say'st thou? Hast thou not a word of joy?	
	Some comfort Nurse.	
Nurse	Faith, here it is.	
	Romeo is banished, and all the world to nothing,	215
	That he dares ne'er come back to challenge you.	
	Or, if he do, it needs must be by stealth.	
	Then, since the case so stands as now it doth,	
	I think it best you married with the County.	
	O he's a lovely gentleman!	220
	Romeo's a dishclout to him. An eagle, madam,	
	Hath not so green, so quick, so fair an eye	
	As Paris hath. Beshrew my very heart,	
	I think you are happy in this second match,	
	For it excels your first. Or if it did not,	225
	Your first is dead, or 'twere as good he were,	
	As living here and you no use of him.	
Juliet	Speakest thou from thy heart?	
Nurse	And from my soul too, or else beshrew them both.	
Juliet	Amen.	230
Nurse	What?	
Juliet	Well, thou hast comforted me marvellous much.	
	Go in, and tell my lady I am gone,	
	Having displeased my father, to Lawrence' cell,	
	To make confession and to be absolved.	235
Nurse	Marry, I will, and this is wisely done.	*Exit.*
Juliet	Ancient damnation! O most wicked fiend!	
	Is it more sin to wish me thus forsworn,	
	Or to dispraise my lord with that same tongue	
	Which she hath praised him with above compare	240
	So many thousand times? Go, counsellor,	
	Thou and my bosom henceforth shall be twain.	
	I'll to the Friar to know his remedy,	
	If all else fail, myself have power to die.	*[Exit.]*

---

195 Nor what is mine … thee good: you'll get no inheritance from me

196 be forsworn: break my word

202 that dim monument where Tybalt lies: Tybalt's tomb

206 My husband is … in heaven: I'm married, I made my vows before God

209 By leaving earth: by dying

210 practise stratagems: play tricks

211 soft: easy

215 all the world to nothing: I bet you anything

216 challenge you: claim you as his wife

217 it needs must be by stealth: it would have to be in secret

219 the County: Paris

221 dishclout: dishcloth

223 Beshrew my very heart: honestly (literal meaning 'curse my heart')

224 happy: lucky

226 'twere as good he were: he might as well be

227 As living … no use of him: he's no use to you if you can't be together

233 my lady: my mother

237 Ancient damnation!: damn you, old woman

238 more sin: more sinful

238 thus forsworn: to break my marriage vows

239 dispraise: be critical of

239 my lord: my husband

240 above compare: as better than anyone

242 Thou and my bosom … be twain: I won't share my thoughts with you again

243 I'll to: I'll go to

243 his remedy: his solution to the problem

244 myself have power to die: I'll find a way to kill myself

A

Juliet and Paris, touring production, 2008.

1 What impression does the body language of the actors give?

2 How well does this fit with the text in this scene? Quote to support your answer.

Dominique Bull, Perri Snowdon

exam SKILLS

Target skill: supporting points with evidence

Question: How does Shakespeare present the relationship between Paris and Juliet in this scene?

In both the extract and essay questions, your points should follow the **P**oint-**E**vidence-**E**xplanation structure.

Find evidence from the text to support the following:

- Paris acts quite arrogantly, and behaves towards Juliet as if she is already his wife
- Juliet's speech is full of double meaning as she attempts to hide her true feelings
- Juliet shows strength of character and self-control
- Paris believes that Juliet has visited the Friar for holy confession.

Now that you have evidence, you should explain each point, looking particularly at the choices about language that Shakespeare makes.

B

Actor's view

Ellie Kendrick
Juliet, summer 2009, on meeting Paris

In this scene Juliet is continuing that double-ness that she has started with the Nurse and her parents, when she has to completely mask her true feelings. And yet she uses words which are semi-true, and she shows an immense power of language and logic, and real quick thinking in this scene, which is just astounding.

So she falls into this rhyme with Paris, this very awkward witty repartee that they have together, when we were playing it, we played it so that Paris thought it was an enjoyable game, and was really getting into it and thought it was funny and witty and a good laugh, whereas Juliet is only just holding onto it, because she has just had the most terrible news, but yet she shows an immense fortitude of character by being able to mask all that. It is interesting the way they fall into this rhyme in this awkward way, because it is almost like a parody of the original interaction between Romeo and Juliet – that beautiful rhyming sonnet that they have together, and here that is deconstructed in a awkward, almost embarrassing, but slightly humorous interchange between Paris and Juliet.

The kiss that they have together, we played that as Paris very confidently believing that he owns Juliet now as his wife-to-be, and just lunges in and goes for it, while she is absolutely terrified and rigid. Almost crying, but trying to mask it, because obviously it is a terrible thing to happen, to be kissed by the man who is potentially going to take you away from the one you are in love with.

ACT 4 SCENE 1

Enter Friar Lawrence and Paris.

Friar Lawrence	On Thursday sir? The time is very short.
Paris	My father Capulet will have it so, And I am nothing slow to slack his haste.
Friar Lawrence	You say you do not know the lady's mind? Uneven is the course, I like it not.
Paris	Immoderately she weeps for Tybalt's death, And therefore have I little talked of love, For Venus smiles not in a house of tears. Now, sir, her father counts it dangerous That she doth give her sorrow so much sway, And in his wisdom hastes our marriage To stop the inundation of her tears, Which, too much minded by herself alone, May be put from her by society. Now do you know the reason of this haste.
Friar Lawrence	*[Aside.]* I would I knew not why it should be slowed. — Look sir, here comes the lady towards my cell.

Enter Juliet.

Paris	Happily met, my lady and my wife.
Juliet	That may be, sir, when I may be a wife.
Paris	That "may be" must be, love, on Thursday next.
Juliet	What "must be" shall be.
Friar Lawrence	That's a certain text.
Paris	Come you to make confession to this father?
Juliet	To answer that, I should confess to you.
Paris	Do not deny to him that you love me.
Juliet	I will confess to you that I love him.
Paris	So will ye, I am sure, that you love me.
Juliet	If I do so, it will be of more price, Being spoke behind your back, than to your face.
Paris	Poor soul, thy face is much abused with tears.
Juliet	The tears have got small victory by that, For it was bad enough before their spite.
Paris	Thou wrong'st it more than tears with that report.
Juliet	That is no slander, sir, which is a truth, And what I spake, I spake it to my face.
Paris	Thy face is mine, and thou hast slandered it.
Juliet	It may be so, for it is not mine own. Are you at leisure, holy father, now, Or shall I come to you at evening mass?

5

10

15

20

25

30

35

3 **I am nothing ... his haste:** I have no reason to want to slow him down

4 **the lady's mind:** what Juliet thinks of it

5 **Uneven is the course:** this is not the normal way to do this

8 **Venus smiles not:** the goddess of love is not happy

9 **counts it:** thinks it is

10 **doth give her sorrow so much sway:** lets her grief overwhelm her

12 **inundation:** flood

13 **too much minded by herself alone:** thought about too much when she's on her own

14 **put from her by society:** pushed aside by company

16 **I would I knew not ... be slowed:** if only I didn't know why it should be delayed

18 **Happily:** fortunately

21 **a certain text:** a saying – that's right

27 **more price:** greater value

29 **much abused with tears:** disfigured by crying

30 **small victory:** hardly any gain

31 **For it was ... their spite:** I wasn't a beauty before they set to work

32 **Thou wrong'st ... with that report:** you do it more harm than the tears, saying that

33 **slander:** untruthful criticism

Friar Lawrence, Juliet with a knife, 2013.

Who do you think was speaking when this photo was taken? Quote from the text to support your answer.

Dickon Tyrrell, Jade Anouka

WHAT I SAY AND WHAT I THINK

- In groups of three, read lines 18–43. One person reads Paris, one person Friar Lawrence, and the third Juliet.
- Read the lines a second time, then say in your own words what your character is really thinking. Is it the same as what you read?

1 What does this activity tell you about Paris and Juliet's relationship at this point?

2 Which words in the extract reveal each character's real emotions?
   - Paris' attempt to kiss Juliet may be:
     - formal (kiss her hand)
     - friendly (a kiss on the cheek)
     - a brief kiss on the lips
     - sexual.
   - Juliet may:
     - avoid or refuse the kiss
     - passively accept the kiss
     - join in.
   - Discuss which best fits what is happening here.

3 If you were directing the play, how would you stage the kiss? Explain your reasons.

4 What is the Friar's role at this point?

5 How does Shakespeare use this incident to show Juliet's character and state of mind?

Actor's view

Colin Hurley
Friar Lawrence, spring 2009

I have to [have a plan] because there's another sobbing teenager on the floor in front of me. She pulls out a knife. She plays the suicide card. So, that puts me in a position where the only card I can play is, 'Well, how about something that is a bit like that – but not.'

So, her emotional state just forced the issue. So I don't think this is something I would do lightly, but it's our only hope. So, there it is, and I'm confident because I've got the big man on my side – because I am a Friar! I'm confident that if she does the right things I can get a letter to lover boy; and okay, it's Plan B but at least they'll be together. The distance will help the emotions to calm down hopefully. There's a saying isn't there, that to really value something, you have to look at it as if for the first time, or as if for the last time. And I think the absence of their daughter will make them appreciate her more.

I didn't want the Friar to be Machiavellian and 'Aha! I'm glad you said that because I have this vial.' So, I did a terrible thing when I – I wasn't sure which vial. I'd got the potion in, 'and take thou...this one, I think it is.' Hoping it was the right one. They need to be improvising.

Actor's view

Ellie Kendrick
Juliet, summer 2009, on suicide

I think that Juliet is completely serious when she suggests that she will commit suicide if she has to marry Paris, simply because Romeo has become her life. Especially as she has abandoned all of her family, she has abandoned everything for him, because he is the sole purpose now of her life and so if she has to leave him, there is no point in going on living for her. I think she is totally serious. I don't think it is just an idle teenage instance of hyperbole, I think it is really serious, and quite terrifying for the Friar, which is why he proposes this mad solution to it – because he really believes her.

Friar Lawrence My leisure serves me, pensive daughter, now.
My lord, we must entreat the time alone. 40

Paris God shield I should disturb devotion.
Juliet, on Thursday early will I rouse ye,
Till then, adieu, and keep this holy kiss.

Exit Paris.

Juliet O shut the door, and when thou hast done so
Come weep with me, past hope, past care, past help. 45

Friar Lawrence O Juliet, I already know thy grief,
It strains me past the compass of my wits.
I hear thou must, and nothing may prorogue it,
On Thursday next be married to this County.

Juliet Tell me not, Friar, that thou hear'st of this, 50
Unless thou tell me how I may prevent it.
If in thy wisdom thou canst give no help,
Do thou but call my resolution wise,
And with this knife, I'll help it presently.
God joined my heart and Romeo's, thou our hands. 55
And ere this hand, by thee to Romeo sealed,
Shall be the label to another deed,
Or my true heart with treacherous revolt
Turn to another, this shall slay them both.
Therefore, out of thy long-experienced time, 60
Give me some present counsel, or behold
'Twixt my extremes and me this bloody knife
Shall play the umpire, arbitrating that
Which the commission of thy years and art
Could to no issue of true honour bring. 65
Be not so long to speak, I long to die,
If what thou speak'st speak not of remedy.

Friar Lawrence Hold daughter, I do spy a kind of hope,
Which craves as desperate an execution
As that is desperate which we would prevent. 70
If, rather than to marry County Paris,
Thou hast the strength of will to slay thyself,
Then is it likely thou wilt undertake
A thing like death, to chide away this shame,
That cop'st with death himself to 'scape from it. 75
And if thou darest, I'll give thee remedy.

Juliet O bid me leap, rather than marry Paris,
From off the battlements of any tower,
Or walk in thievish ways, or bid me lurk
Where serpents are. Chain me with roaring bears, 80
Or hide me nightly in a charnel-house,
O'er-covered quite with dead men's rattling bones,
With reeky shanks and yellow chapless skulls.
Or bid me go into a new-made grave
And hide me with a dead man in his shroud, 85
(Things that to hear them told have made me tremble),

39 My leisure serves me: I'm free
39 pensive: double meaning: thoughtful; sad
39 daughter: he is her spiritual father
40 entreat the time alone: need to be alone
41 shield: forbid
42 rouse: wake
45 care: spiritual help
47 It strains me past the compass of my wits: I can't think of an answer
48 prorogue: postpone
53 Do thou but call my resolution wise: just say I'm making the right decision
54 I'll help it presently: I'll carry it out now
56 ere: before
57 Shall be the label to another deed: will be given to another man in marriage
58 true: faithful
59 this: the knife
59 them both: her hand and heart
60 time: life
61 present counsel: advice, now
62 'Twixt: between
62 my extremes: my appalling situation
63–5 arbitrating that ... honour bring: providing the answer that you, for all your experience, cannot give
67 speak not of remedy: doesn't give an answer
68 Hold: wait
69–70 Which craves ... we would prevent: which will take as much courage as killing yourself
74 A thing like death: something similar to death
74 chide away: drive away
74 this shame: marrying Paris
75 That cop'st with ... 'scape from it: if you can face the idea of death to escape it
79 thievish ways: dangerous places full of thieves
81 charnel-house: a place where bones were stored when graves were re-used for more recent burials
83 reeky shanks: smelly shinbones
83 chapless: missing the lower jaw

Friar Lawrence, 2004.

Which line or lines do you think Friar Lawrence was speaking when this photo was taken? Quote the line or lines and explain your reasons.

John McEnery

exam SKILLS

Target skill: analysing Shakespeare's craft

To address AO2 (Language, structure and form), you need to remember that the play is not real but Shakespeare's creation. As playwright, Shakespeare has constructed the events, their order, the characters' behaviour and their words, and you are analysing his craft.

- Shakespeare told us in the Prologue that "A pair of star-crossed lovers take their life" but here, the Friar manages to "spy a kind of hope". *What effect do you think this has on the audience?*
- Shakespeare takes time to explain the powerful effects of the drug. *These details appear just to tell us about the drug itself, but more importantly, what is Shakespeare telling us about Juliet?*
- Shakespeare uses the Friar's speech to tell us how the lovers could be reunited. *How far do we expect this to happen?*

Director's Note, 4.1

✔ Paris tells Friar Lawrence he is to marry Juliet in three days (Thursday).
✔ Juliet arrives, and is uncomfortable as Paris treats her as his love.
✔ Paris leaves so Juliet can confess to the Friar.
✔ Juliet is desperate, and threatens suicide; Friar Lawrence comes up with a plan:
  ● Juliet is to go home and agree to marry Paris
  ● but on Wednesday night she must make sure the Nurse does not sleep in her room, and she will take a drug Friar Lawrence gives her, which will make her seem dead
  ● she will be in a coma for 42 hours, long enough to be buried in the Capulet vault
  ● Friar Lawrence and Romeo will be there when she wakes, and she and Romeo can go off in exile together.
✔ Who benefits from the Friar's plan?

	And I will do it without fear or doubt,	
	To live an unstained wife to my sweet love.	88 **unstained:** faithful
Friar Lawrence	Hold then. Go home, be merry, give consent	
	To marry Paris. Wednesday is tomorrow, — 90	
	Tomorrow night look that thou lie alone,	91 **look that thou lie:** make sure you sleep
	Let not thy nurse lie with thee in thy chamber.	
	Take thou this vial, being then in bed,	93 **vial:** very small bottle
	And this distilling liquor drink thou off,	94 **distilling liquor:** strong liquid
		94 **drink thou off:** drink up completely
	When presently through all thy veins shall run — 95	95 **When presently:** at once
	A cold and drowsy humour. For no pulse	96 **A cold and drowsy humour:** a feeling of cold and sleepiness
	Shall keep his native progress, but surcease.	96–7 **For no pulse ... but surcease:** your pulse will seem to stop
	No warmth, no breath, shall testify thou livest,	
	The roses in thy lips and cheeks shall fade	
	To many ashes, thy eyes' windows fall — 100	100 **many:** pale
	Like death when he shuts up the day of life.	
	Each part, deprived of supple government,	102 **supple government:** the power to move
	Shall stiff and stark and cold appear like death,	
	And in this borrowed likeness of shrunk death	104 **borrowed likeness:** imitation
	Thou shalt continue two and forty hours, — 105	
	And then awake as from a pleasant sleep.	
	Now when the bridegroom in the morning comes	
	To rouse thee from thy bed, there art thou dead.	
	Then, as the manner of our country is,	109 **as the manner of our country is:** in the way we do things here
	In thy best robes uncovered on the bier, — 110	110 **bier:** the moveable stand a body is carried to the grave on
	Thou shalt be borne to that same ancient vault	111 **vault:** tomb
	Where all the kindred of the Capulets lie.	
	In the mean time, against thou shalt awake,	113 **against thou shalt wake:** in preparation for when you wake
	Shall Romeo by my letters know our drift,	114 **our drift:** what we have planned
	And hither shall he come, and he and I — 115	
	Will watch thy waking, and that very night	
	Shall Romeo bear thee hence to Mantua.	117 **bear thee hence:** take you away
	And this shall free thee from this present shame,	
	If no inconstant toy nor womanish fear,	119 **inconstant toy:** childish change of mind
	Abate thy valour in the acting it. — 120	120 **Abate thy valour:** weaken your courage
Juliet	Give me, give me! O, tell not me of fear!	122 **prosperous:** lucky
Friar Lawrence	Hold, get you gone, be strong and prosperous	
	In this resolve. I'll send a friar with speed	
	To Mantua with my letters to thy lord.	
Juliet	Love give me strength and strength shall help afford. — 125	125 **shall help afford:** will provide my help
	Farewell, dear father. *They exit.*	

ACT 4 SCENE 2

Enter Capulet, Lady Capulet, Nurse, and Servants.

Capulet	So many guests invite as here are writ. *[Exit a Servant.]*	1 **So many guests ... here are writ:** here's a list of the guests to be invited
	Sirrah, go hire me twenty cunning cooks.	2 **cunning:** skilful
Servant	You shall have none ill, sir, for I'll try if they can lick their fingers.	3 **none ill:** no bad ones
Capulet	How canst thou try them so? — 5	3–4 **try if they can lick their fingers:** test them to see if they lick their fingers (good cooks were supposed to do so)
Servant	Marry sir, 'tis an ill cook that cannot lick his own	

Juliet, summer 2009.

1 What line(s) has Juliet just spoken? Explain why your choice fits the image.

2 We can't see who Juliet is looking at. Who is it? Give reasons for your answer.

3 How would this scene appear to:

   a) Shakespeare's original audiences?

   b) an audience today?

Ellie Kendrick

Director's Note, 4.2

✔ Capulet is organising the wedding feast.

✔ Juliet returns, apologises, and says she will marry Paris.

✔ Overjoyed, Capulet moves the wedding forward to Wednesday.

✔ How close to the truth is Juliet's speech about Paris?

	fingers. Therefore he that cannot lick his fingers goes not with me.
Capulet	Go, be gone. *[Exit Servants.]*
	We shall be much unfurnished for this time. —
	What, is my daughter gone to Friar Lawrence?
Nurse	Ay forsooth.
Capulet	Well, he may chance to do some good on her.
	A peevish self-willed harlotry it is. *Enter Juliet.*
Nurse	See where she comes from shrift with merry look.
Capulet	How now, my headstrong, where have you been gadding?
Juliet	Where I have learnt me to repent the sin
	Of disobedient opposition
	To you and your behests, and am enjoined
	By holy Lawrence to fall prostrate here,
	And beg your pardon. Pardon, I beseech you,
	Henceforward I am ever ruled by you.
Capulet	Send for the County, go tell him of this.
	I'll have this knot knit up tomorrow morning.
Juliet	I met the youthful lord at Lawrence' cell,
	And gave him what becomèd love I might,
	Not stepping o'er the bounds of modesty.
Capulet	Why, I am glad on't. This is well. Stand up.
	This is as't should be. Let me see the County.
	Ay, marry, go I say, and fetch him hither.
	Now, afore God, this reverend holy friar,
	Our whole city is much bound to him.
Juliet	Nurse, will you go with me into my closet,
	To help me sort such needful ornaments
	As you think fit to furnish me tomorrow?
Lady Capulet	No, not till Thursday; there is time enough.
Capulet	Go, Nurse, go with her. We'll to church tomorrow.

Exit Juliet and Nurse.

Lady Capulet	We shall be short in our provision,
	'Tis now near night.
Capulet	Tush, I will stir about,
	And all things shall be well, I warrant thee, wife:
	Go thou to Juliet, help to deck up her;
	I'll not to bed tonight; let me alone;
	I'll play the housewife for this once. What, ho!
	They are all forth. Well, I will walk myself
	To County Paris, to prepare up him
	Against tomorrow. My heart is wondrous light,
	Since this same wayward girl is so reclaimed. *Exit all.*

Line numbers (right margin): 10, 15, 20, 25, 30, 35, 40, 45

10 **We shall be … for this time:** we won't be ready in time
12 **Ay forsooth:** yes, indeed
14 **A peevish self-willed harlotry it is:** she's a moody, stubborn little madam
15 **shrift:** confession
16 **my headstrong:** my stubborn child
16 **gadding:** wandering off to
19 **behests:** commands
19 **enjoined:** instructed
20 **fall prostrate:** throw myself at your feet
22 **Henceforward:** from now on
22 **I am ever ruled:** I will always obey
24 **this knot:** the marriage
25 **the youthful lord:** Paris
26 **gave him what becomèd love I might:** showed him as much love as was suitable
32 **is much bound to him:** owes him a great deal
33 **closet:** private room
34 **sort:** choose
34 **needful:** necessary
35 **fit to furnish me:** suitable to wear
38 **shall be short in our provision:** won't have enough food and drink
39 **Tush:** don't be foolish
39 **stir about:** get it done
40 **warrant:** promise
41 **deck up her:** choose what she'll wear
42 **let me alone:** let me deal with it
44 **forth:** out of the house
45-6 **prepare up him Against tomorrow:** tell him the wedding's now tomorrow
47 **reclaimed:** obedient, my favourite again

SHAKESPEARE'S WORLD

Beds

The Chamberlain's Men would not have used as many props as a modern theatre company. Many of the major props which they did have are used in *Romeo and Juliet*. There are the swords (for the fight scenes) and the torches (to help the audience imagine the dark). In this scene the company's biggest prop was used: the bed.

Sometimes the bed was used behind doors or curtains at the back of the stage, which were opened to show it. We call this a 'discovery'. On other occasions, the bed was pushed onto the stage itself. In this scene, a 'discovery' allows Juliet to be found by the Nurse, but the dramatic impact would be greater if the bed is on stage.

Shakespeare used the bed in a number of other plays, including *Othello*, and *Henry IV Part 2*.

FROM THE REHEARSAL ROOM...

POWER WORDS

This activity looks at Juliet's soliloquy (lines 14–57). Work in groups of four. Each member of the group is given a section of several lines, ending at the end of a sentence.

- Choose three words that seem most important in your lines. These 'power words' can be any words you like. For example, from the first line you could choose "faint", "fear" and "veins".

- The group reads the passage out loud, each person just saying the 'power' words, not the whole line.

- Now read the passage again. This time, each person reads all of their lines, giving special emphasis to the 'power' words.

1 What kind of words have people chosen?

2 What themes do the words highlight in the soliloquy?

3 What type of sounds and atmosphere do the words create?

4 What might the 'power' words tell you about Juliet's thoughts and feelings at the beginning, middle and end of her soliloquy?

5 How does Shakespeare use the language he chooses to give Juliet in this soliloquy to communicate her mood to the audience?

Juliet during her soliloquy, 2013.

The plan is working. Why have the director and actor chosen to have Juliet looking scared?

Jade Anouka

Enter Juliet and Nurse, a bed with curtains on stage.

Juliet   Ay, those attires are best. But gentle nurse
I pray thee leave me to myself tonight.
For I have need of many orisons
To move the heavens to smile upon my state,
Which, well thou know'st, is cross and full of sin.   5

Enter Lady Capulet.

Lady Capulet   What, are you busy, ho? Need you my help?

Juliet   No madam, we have cull'd such necessaries
As are behoveful for our state tomorrow.
So please you, let me now be left alone,
And let the Nurse this night sit up with you,   10
For I am sure you have your hands full all
In this so sudden business.

Lady Capulet   Good night.
Get thee to bed and rest for thou hast need.

Exit Lady Capulet and Nurse.

Juliet   Farewell. God knows when we shall meet again.
I have a faint cold fear thrills through my veins   15
That almost freezes up the heat of life.
I'll call them back again to comfort me.
Nurse! — What should she do here?
My dismal scene I needs must act alone.
Come vial. What if this mixture do not work at all?   20
Shall I be married then tomorrow morning?
[Taking out a dagger.]
No, no, this shall forbid it. Lie thou there.
What if it be a poison, which the Friar
Subtly hath ministered to have me dead,
Lest in this marriage he should be dishonoured,   25
Because he married me before to Romeo?
I fear it is, and yet methinks it should not,
For he hath still been tried a holy man.
How, if when I am laid into the tomb,
I wake before the time that Romeo   30
Come to redeem me? There's a fearful point.
Shall I not, then, be stifled in the vault,
To whose foul mouth no healthsome air breathes in,
And there die strangled ere my Romeo comes?
Or if I live, is it not very like   35
The horrible conceit of death and night,
Together with the terror of the place,
As in a vault, an ancient receptacle,
Where for this many hundred years the bones
Of all my buried ancestors are packed,   40
Where bloody Tybalt, yet but green in earth,
Lies festering in his shroud, where, as they say,
At some hours in the night spirits resort —

1 **attires:** clothes
3 **orisons:** prayers
4 **state:** circumstances
5 **cross:** unfavourable, not what I want
5 **full of sin:** because she's married already

7 **cull'd:** picked out
8 **behoveful:** needed
8 **state:** ceremony

15 **faint cold fear:** a fear that makes me feel cold and close to fainting

18 **What should she do here?:** what use could she be?
19 **dismal:** disastrous, fatal
20 **vial:** very small bottle

24 **Subtly hath ministered:** has cunningly given me
25 **Lest in ... be dishonoured:** in case he's found out and disgraced at the wedding
28 **still been tried:** always been shown to be
29 **How, if:** what if

31 **redeem:** save, rescue
32 **stifled:** suffocated
33 **healthsome:** fresh, healthy
34 **strangled:** choked, dead from lack of air
34 **ere:** before
36 **The horrible conceit of death and night:** the awful thoughts of death and darkness

41 **yet but green in earth:** only recently buried

43 **resort:** meet in

95

Alack, alack, is it not like that I,
So early waking, what with loathsome smells,   45
And shrieks like mandrakes torn out of the earth,
That living mortals, hearing them, run mad —
O if I wake, shall I not be distraught,
Environéd with all these hideous fears.
And madly play with my forefather's joints,   50
And pluck the mangled Tybalt from his shroud,
And in this rage, with some great kinsman's bone,
As with a club, dash out my desp'rate brains?
O look, methinks I see my cousin's ghost
Seeking out Romeo that did spit his body   55
Upon a rapier's point. Stay, Tybalt, stay!
Romeo, Romeo, Romeo, here's drink. I drink to thee!

She drinks, and falls on the bed, within the curtains.

44 **is it not like:** isn't it likely
46 **mandrakes:** plants said to scream when pulled up, causing those who heard the screams to go mad and die
49 **Environéd with:** surrounded by
52 **rage:** madness
55 **spit:** skewer
56 **stay!:** stop!

Director's Note, 4.3

✔ Lady Capulet and the Nurse leave Juliet alone for the night.
✔ Juliet is scared. She worries what might happen – if the drug does not work, if Friar Lawrence has actually given her poison, if she wakes too early...
✔ She takes the drug.
✔ What effect will the soliloquy have on the audience?

exam PREPARATION

Text focus: Act 4 Scene 3 lines 15–57

(AO1) Response to characters and events:
- When the need for comfort almost overwhelms her, Juliet starts to call for the Nurse, not for her mother. *Why do you think she calls for the Nurse's comfort after being let down by her in Act 3 Scene 5?*
- Juliet runs through the possible problems in her mind and verbalises them for the audience. Her fears remind us of both her youth and her maturity. *Find evidence of both.*
- Juliet has a dagger with her in case the drugs don't work. *Do you think that she would commit suicide?*
- The eventual decision to drink the draught comes quite suddenly, provoked by the image of Tybalt's ghost seeking out Romeo for vengeance. *Why do you think she drinks the draught at this point?*
- Arrange these events in the order they take place in the soliloquy:
  1 Juliet fears being suffocated by the vault's stale air.
  2 Juliet fears seeing her ancestors' ghosts in the vault.
  3 She imagines Tybalt's ghost trying to kill Romeo.
  4 Juliet feels cold with fear.
  5 She wants company, before realising this is a task that she can only do alone.
  6 Juliet fears that the draught is a poison to kill her.

(AO2) Language, structure and form:
- The speech is a soliloquy, outlining Juliet's fears. *Why might Shakespeare have chosen to give her a soliloquy here rather than just continuing the play's action?*
- Read lines 15–16. *Which words evoke anxiety and cold? What do they reveal about Juliet's state of mind?*
- Juliet uses the interrogative mood (questions) then moves to an exclamatory mood towards the end. *Find examples and comment on the effect created.*
- Look at the sentence length of lines 35–49. *What effect does this create?*
- Shakespeare evokes the terror of the Capulet tomb by giving us, through Juliet's imagination, images of dead bodies. *Find examples and comment on what they convey about Juliet's state of mind.*

Question:
How does Shakespeare present Juliet in this part of the play? (15 marks)

Advice: Linking character points to wider thematic issues in the play can help to strengthen your answers. *Consider in what ways this extract tells us more about the themes of:*
- *love,* • *death,* • *parents and children,* • *power.*

Enter Lady Capulet and Nurse.

Lady Capulet   Hold, take these keys and fetch more spices, Nurse.

Nurse   They call for dates and quinces in the pastry.

Enter Capulet.

Capulet   Come, stir, stir, stir! The second cock hath crowed,
The curfew-bell hath rung, 'tis three o'clock.
Look to the baked meats, good Angelica,   5
Spare not for the cost.

Nurse   Go you cot-quean, go,
Get you to bed. Faith, you'll be sick tomorrow
For this night's watching.

Capulet   No, not a whit. What? I have watched ere now
All night for less cause, and ne'er been sick.   10

Lady Capulet   Ay, you have been a mouse-hunt in your time;
But I will watch you from such watching now.

Exit Lady Capulet and Nurse.

Capulet   A jealous hood, a jealous hood!
Enter three or four servants with cooking-spits, logs and baskets.
Now, fellow, what's there?

First Servant   Things for the cook, sir, but I know not what.   15

Capulet   Make haste, make haste.   *[Exit First Servant.]*
Sirrah, fetch drier logs.
Call Peter, he will show thee where they are.

Second Servant   I have a head, sir, that will find out logs,
And never trouble Peter for the matter.   *He exits.*

Capulet   Mass and well said, a merry whoreson, ha!   20
Thou shalt be logger-head. Good faith, 'tis day. *Music offstage.*
The County will be here with music straight,
For so he said he would, I hear him near.
Nurse! Wife! What ho? What, Nurse, I say!
Enter Nurse.   Go waken Juliet, go and trim her up.   25
I'll go and chat with Paris. Hie, make haste,
Make haste, the bridegroom he is come already.
Make haste I say.   *Exit Capulet.*

2 **pastry:** room where pastry was made

4 **curfew-bell:** bell rung in the early morning when the watchmen went off duty and the gates were unlocked

5 **Angelica:** the name of a female servant in the room, or the Nurse

6 **Spare not for:** don't hold back because of

6 **cot-quean:** man who interferes in women's business of running the house

8 **watching:** staying awake

9 **not a whit:** not in the slightest

11 **mouse-hunt:** woman-chaser

12 **watch you from such watching:** keep an eye on you to stop that

13 **hood:** woman

20 **Mass:** short for 'by the Mass'; an oath

20 **merry whoreson:** cheerful bastard

21 **logger-head:** double meaning: chief log fetcher; a blockhead/fool

22 **straight:** any minute

25 **trim her up:** get her dressed

Director's Note, 4.4

✔ The Capulets are up all night preparing for the feast.

✔ When he hears Paris' musicians coming, Capulet sends the Nurse to wake Juliet.

✔ Why might Shakespeare have followed Juliet's soliloquy with this scene?

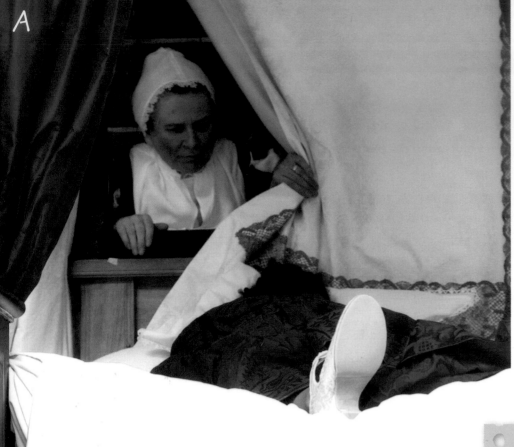

A

B

The Nurse discovers Juliet

Although the story was set 200 years before, we believe Shakespeare's company played it in 'modern dress' for their time. Here it is in Elizabethan dress (A) and modern dress (B). Which do you think is closest to Shakespeare's intention?

A, 2004, Bette Bourne, Kananu Kirimi; B, 2013, Jade Anouka, Lisa Stevenson.

ACT 4 SCENE 5

[The Nurse goes to the bed.]

Nurse	Mistress, what mistress? Juliet? Fast, I warrant her, she.
	— Why lamb, why lady? Fie, you slugabed!
	Why love I say? Madam? Sweetheart? Why bride?
	What, not a word? You take your pennyworths now.
	Sleep for a week, for the next night, I warrant,
	The County Paris hath set up his rest
	That you shall rest but little, God forgive me.
	— Marry, and amen, how sound is she asleep?
	I needs must wake her. Madam, madam, madam!
	Ay, let the County take you in your bed,
	He'll fright you up, i' faith. Will it not be?

[She opens the bed curtains.]

	What, dressed, and in your clothes, and down again?
	I must needs wake you. Lady, lady, lady?
	Alas, alas! Help, help! My lady's dead!
	O wereaday, that ever I was born!
	Some *aqua vitae*, ho! My lord! My lady!

Enter Lady Capulet.

Lady Capulet	What noise is here?
Nurse	O lamentable day!
Lady Capulet	What is the matter?
Nurse	Look, look. O heavy day!
Lady Capulet	O me, O me, my child, my only life.
	Revive, look up, or I will die with thee!
	Help, help! Call help! *Enter Capulet.*
Capulet	For shame, bring Juliet forth, her lord is come.
Nurse	She's dead. Deceased. She's dead. Alack the day!
Lady Capulet	Alack the day, she's dead, she's dead, she's dead!
Capulet	Ha! Let me see her. Out, alas, she's cold:
	Her blood is settled and her joints are stiff.
	Life and these lips have long been separated.
	Death lies on her like an untimely frost
	Upon the sweetest flower of all the field.
Nurse	O lamentable day!
Lady Capulet	O woeful time!
Capulet	Death, that hath ta'en her hence to make me wail,
	Ties up my tongue, and will not let me speak.

Enter Friar Lawrence and County Paris with Musicians.

Friar Lawrence	Come, is the bride ready to go to church?
Capulet	Ready to go, but never to return.
	O son, the night before thy wedding day
	Hath Death lain with thy wife. There she lies,

Line notes:

1 **Fast:** fast asleep

4 **take your pennyworths now:** sleep while you can

6 **set up his rest:** decided

10 **take you:** double meaning: arrive and find you; have sex with you

11 **fright you up:** startle you awake

12 **dressed, and in ... down again:** dressed, and then gone back to sleep in your clothes

13 **I must needs:** I really have to

15 **wereaday:** alas

16 *aqua vitae:* brandy

18 **heavy:** unhappy

19 **my only life:** the only child I have

26 **is settled:** isn't moving round her body

28 **untimely:** coming at the wrong time, out of season

31 **ta'en her hence:** taken her away

36 **lain with:** slept with

99

Friar Lawrence, the Capulets and Paris weep over Juliet in the background, 2013.

At this moment Friar Lawrence and the audience share a secret unknown to the others on stage. Shakespeare does this in many plays. Why might this be attractive to him as a playwright?

l-r: Dickon Tyrrell, Jason Baughan, Jade Anouka, Emma Pallant, Tom Whitelock.

exam SKILLS

Target skill: understanding dramatic irony

Dramatic irony is when the significance of the characters' actions or words is clear to the audience but not to the characters. Shakespeare utilises dramatic irony to heighten tension, particularly here, when the characters believe that Juliet is dead but the audience know that she isn't.

Use the **P**oint, **E**vidence, **E**xplanation structure to answer the following questions.

1 How does Capulet react to Juliet's death?
2 How does Lady Capulet react to Juliet's death?
3 How does Paris react to Juliet's death?
4 Are the Friar's words are deliberately deceitful?
5 How does Shakespeare use dramatic irony in this scene?

SHAKESPEARE'S WORLD

Funeral customs

Church bells were rung to tell people someone had died. Until the funeral, Elizabethans usually watched beside the corpse day and night, both as a mark of respect and to keep the corpse safe. In England the body was usually buried within two or three days of death, but in the world of the play, Juliet's funeral must be the same day or the next day. In simple funerals a few family members carried the body to be buried. As in the play, wealthy families often had their own large family tomb in the churchyard. More elaborate funerals had a horse-drawn carriage draped in black cloth, and many more mourners. As with weddings, local people watched funerals. The corpses of wealthy and important people were dressed in expensive clothes and ornaments. At the grave, people threw sprigs of rosemary, the herb of remembrance, onto the body. Afterwards there was a funeral feast.

	Flower as she was, deflowered by him.
	Death is my son-in-law, Death is my heir,
	My daughter he hath wedded. I will die,
	And leave him all. Life, living, all is Death's.
Paris	Have I thought long to see this morning's face,
	And doth it give me such a sight as this?
Lady Capulet	Accursed, unhappy, wretched, hateful day!
	Most miserable hour that e'er time saw
	In lasting labour of his pilgrimage.
	But one, poor one, one poor and loving child,
	But one thing to rejoice and solace in,
	And cruel Death hath catched it from my sight!
Nurse	O woe! O woeful, woeful, woeful day!
	Most lamentable day, most woeful day,
	That ever, ever, I did yet behold!
	O day, O day, O day, O hateful day,
	Never was seen so black a day as this.
	O woeful day, O woeful day!
Paris	Beguiled, divorcèd, wrongèd, spited, slain!
	Most detestable Death, by thee beguiled,
	By cruel, cruel thee quite overthrown.
	O love, O life! Not life, but love in death!
Capulet	Despised, distressèd, hated, martyred, killed!
	Uncomfortable time, why cam'st thou now
	To murder, murder our solemnity?
	O child, O child! My soul and not my child,
	Dead art thou! Alack my child is dead,
	And with my child, my joys are buried.
Friar Lawrence	Peace, ho, for shame! Confusion's cure lives not
	In these confusions. Heaven and yourself
	Had part in this fair maid, now heaven hath all,
	And all the better is it for the maid.
	Your part in her you could not keep from death,
	But heaven keeps his part in eternal life.
	The most you sought was her promotion,
	For 'twas your heaven she should be advanced,
	And weep ye now, seeing she is advanced
	Above the clouds, as high as heaven itself?
	O in this love, you love your child so ill
	That you run mad, seeing that she is well.
	She's not well married, that lives married long,
	But she's best married, that dies married young.
	Dry up your tears, and stick your rosemary
	On this fair corse, and, as the custom is,
	And in her best array, bear her to church.
	For though fond nature bids us all lament,
	Yet nature's tears are reason's merriment.
Capulet	All things that we ordainèd festival,
	Turn from their office to black funeral.
	Our instruments to melancholy bells,

37 deflowered by him: her virginity taken by Death

41 Have I thought long ... morning's face: I've waited so impatiently for this morning

45 In lasting labour of his pilgrimage: on the long hard journey of all those years
47 solace in: take comfort from
48 hath catched it: has snatched this child

55 Beguiled: cheated
60 Uncomfortable: without comfort
61 murder our solemnity: kill her and so kill our celebration
65-6 Confusion's cure ... these confusions: we can't sort things out until we all calm down
67 Had part in: shared
69 Your part: the mortal part (her body)
70 his part: her soul
71 her promotion: social advancement (through marriage)
72 'twas your heaven she should be advanced: the best you could imagine for her was to marry well
75-6 O in this love ... that she is well: you love your child so little that you go mad with grief despite the fact she's in the best possible place
77-8 She's not well married ... dies married young: she's better off dying young and going to heaven than marrying well here
79 rosemary: herb of remembrance, used at funerals
80 corse: corpse
81 array: clothes and ornaments
82 fond nature: foolish natural feeling
83 nature's tears are reason's merriment: our natural sorrow should really, if we think about it, be joy
84 things we ordainèd festival: wedding preparations
85 office: intended use
85 to black funeral: to serve her funeral

101

Our wedding cheer to a sad burial feast,
Our solemn hymns to sullen dirges change,
Our bridal flowers serve for a buried corse,
And all things change them to the contrary. 90

88 sullen dirges: gloomy funeral hymns
90 contrary: opposite

Friar Lawrence Sir, go you in, and madam, go with him,
And go Sir Paris, every one prepare
To follow this fair corse unto her grave.
The heavens do lour upon you for some ill,
Move them no more by crossing their high will. 95

94 lour: frown

Exit Capulet, Lady Capulet, Paris, and Friar Lawrence, each putting rosemary on the body, and shutting the bed curtains.

First Musician Faith, we may put up our pipes and be gone.

96 may put up our pipes and be gone: might as well pack up our instruments and go

Nurse Honest goodfellows, ah, put up, put up,
For well you know, this is a pitiful case.

98 pitiful case: very sad situation

First Musician Ay, by my troth, the case may be amended.

99 the case may be amended: double meaning: the situation could be improved; his music case needs mending

Exit Nurse, the Musicians start to follow.
Enter Peter.

Peter Musicians, O musicians, "Heart's ease, Heart's ease": O, 100
and you will have me live, play "Heart's ease".

First Musician Why "Heart's ease"?

Peter O, musicians, because my heart itself plays "My heart
is full of woe": O play me some merry dump to comfort
me. 105

104 merry dump: cheerful, sad song (which would be impossible)

First Musician Not a dump we, 'tis no time to play now.

Peter You will not then?

First Musician No.

Peter I will then give it you soundly.

First Musician What will you give us? 110

Peter No money, on my faith, but the gleek. I will give you
the minstrel.

111 the gleek: I'll mock you
111-2 I will give you the minstrel: I'll call you minstrels (wandering beggars that usually played music badly)

First Musician Then I will give you the serving-creature.

Peter Then will I lay the serving-creature's dagger on your
pate. I will carry no crotchets, I'll *re* you, I'll *fa* you. Do 115
you note me?

113 the serving-creature: suggesting Peter is a bad servant
115 pate: head
115 I will carry no crotchets: double meaning: I won't put up with your nonsense; I won't put up with your music. Start of a run of musical puns

First Musician An you *re* us, and *fa* us, you note us.

Second Musician Pray you put up your dagger and put out your wit.
Then have at you with my wit.

118 put up: put away
118 put out your wit: show some sense

Peter I will dry-beat you with an iron wit, and put up my iron 120
dagger. Answer me like men:
  When griping grief the heart doth wound,
  And doleful dumps the mind oppress,
  Then music with her silver sound
Why "silver sound"? Why "music with her silver sound"? 125
What say you, Simon Catling?

120 dry-beat you with an iron wit: I'll use my sharp wit to beat you without drawing blood
126 Catling: named after a string for a musical instrument made from catgut

102

First Musician	Marry, sir, because silver hath a sweet sound.
Peter	Prates. What say you, Hugh Rebeck?
Second Musician	I say "silver sound", because musicians sound for silver.
Peter	Prates too. What say you, James Soundpost? 130
Third Musician	Faith, I know not what to say.
Peter	O I cry you mercy, you are the singer, I will say for you. It is "music with her silver sound", because musicians have no gold for sounding.
	Then music with her silver sound, 135
	With speedy help doth lend redress. *Exit Peter.*
First Musician	What a pestilent knave is this same!
Second Musician	Hang him, Jack! Come, we'll in here, tarry for the mourners, and stay dinner. *They exit.*

ACT 5 SCENE 1

Enter Romeo.

Romeo	If I may trust the flattering truth of sleep,
	My dreams presage some joyful news at hand.
	My bosom's lord sits lightly in his throne.
	And all this day an unaccustomed spirit
	Lifts me above the ground with cheerful thoughts.
	I dreamt my lady came and found me dead
	(Strange dream that gives a dead man leave to think.)
	And breathed such life with kisses in my lips,
	That I revived and was an emperor.
	Ah me, how sweet is love itself possessed, 10
	When but love's shadows are so rich in joy!
	Enter Balthasar, Romeo's servant, in riding boots.
	News from Verona. How now Balthasar?
	Dost thou not bring me letters from the Friar?
	How doth my lady? Is my father well?
	How doth my lady Juliet? That I ask again, 15
	For nothing can be ill, if she be well.
Balthasar	Then she is well, and nothing can be ill.
	Her body sleeps in Capel's monument,
	And her immortal part with angels lives.
	I saw her laid low in her kindred's vault,
	And presently took post to tell it you. 20
	O pardon me for bringing these ill news,
	Since you did leave it for my office, sir.
Romeo	Is it even so? Then I deny you, stars. —
	Thou know'st my lodging, get me ink and paper, 25
	And hire post-horses, I will hence tonight.
Balthasar	I do beseech you, sir, have patience.
	Your looks are pale and wild, and do import
	Some misadventure.
Romeo	Tush, thou art deceived.
	Leave me, and do the thing I bid thee do. 30

ACT 5 SCENE 1

127 **silver hath a sweet sound:** when given in payment

128 **Prates:** nonsense

128 **Rebeck:** a type of violin

129 **sound for silver:** play music for money

130 **Soundpost:** part of a violin

132 **you are the singer:** you sing, you don't 'say' (talk)

136 *doth lend redress:* puts things right

137 **What a pestilent knave is this same:** he's a pain in the neck

138 **tarry:** hang around

139 **stay:** wait for

Director's Note, 4.5

✔ The Nurse finds Juliet, and believes she is dead.

✔ She calls the Capulets, who are grief-stricken.

✔ Paris arrives with his musicians; he too becomes distraught.

✔ Friar Lawrence tells them to rejoice because she has gone to heaven, and starts to arrange the funeral.

✔ Afterwards, Peter jokes with the musicians.

1 **the flattering truth of sleep:** what my dreams tell me

2 **presage:** predict

3 **bosom's lord:** heart

4 **unaccustomed spirit:** unusual cheerfulness

7 **leave:** permission

10 **itself possessed:** experienced in reality

11 **but love's shadows:** just dreams of love

18 **Capel's monument:** the Capulet tomb

19 **immortal part:** soul

21 **presently took post:** set off as fast as possible on a relay of hired horses

23 **Since you did leave it for my office:** but when you left you told me to bring news

24 **Is it even so?:** so that's what's happened

24 **I deny you, stars:** I won't accept the influence of the stars on events

26 **post-horses:** horses hired from inns, used to travel long distances quickly, by changing tired horses at other post inns

28–9 **do import Some misadventure:** nothing good can come of acting now

29 **Tush:** don't be foolish **103**

SHAKESPEARE'S WORLD

◇◇◇◇◇◇◇◇◇◇◇

What was an apothecary?

An apothecary was someone who made and prescribed medicine, similar to a chemist today. Apothecaries also sold spices, plants, oils, chemicals, and the ingredients for cosmetics and perfumes.

Doctors were expensive in Shakespeare's time, so people often went to apothecaries for treatment. Many apothecaries had some medical training, but they were not seen as professional people. Doctors were. So apothecaries charged a fee, but could not charge as much as doctors. Sometimes priests or monks treated poor people for free, using similar medicines. In *Romeo and Juliet* Friar Lawrence clearly makes herbal medicines. Apothecaries often first prescribed vinegar to patients to prevent infection. Other medicines included arsenic, sage, dried toad, lavender, rose, bay leaf, wormwood, liquorice and mint. It was against the law to sell poison, as the apothecary in this scene tells Romeo. However, apothecaries had access to various poisonous substances and people were prepared to pay a lot for poison.

Director's view

Bill Buckhurst
Director, spring 2009

What we've discovered is that when Romeo leaves his fate with the stars, he's constantly going 'you be my guide', he believes in a larger power than himself which is guiding him on life's journey. And then when he's told the news of Juliet's death he says, 'I defy you stars', another pivotal point in the play. He suddenly comes of age and takes responsibility for his own actions, and what does he do? He goes and kills himself.

The Apothecary and Romeo, 2013.

1 Which line do you think the Apothecary was speaking when this photo was taken? Give reasons for your answer.

2 Shakespeare doesn't make the Apothecary grateful for Romeo's custom. Why might he have chosen to do this?

Beruce Khan, Will Featherstone

	Hast thou no letters to me from the Friar?
Balthasar	No, my good lord.
Romeo	No matter. Get thee gone,

And hire those horses, I'll be with thee straight.
Well, Juliet, I will lie with thee tonight.   *Exit Balthasar.*
Let's see for means. O mischief, thou art swift   35
To enter in the thoughts of desperate men.
I do remember an apothecary,
And hereabouts 'a dwells, which late I noted
In tattered weeds, with overwhelming brows,
Culling of simples. Meagre were his looks,   40
Sharp misery had worn him to the bones.
And in his needy shop a tortoise hung,
An alligator stuffed, and other skins
Of ill-shaped fishes. And about his shelves
A beggarly account of empty boxes,   45
Green earthen pots, bladders, and musty seeds,
Remnants of packthread, and old cakes of roses
Were thinly scattered, to make up a show.
Noting this penury, to myself I said,
"An if a man did need a poison now,   50
Whose sale is present death in Mantua,
Here lives a caitiff wretch would sell it him."
O this same thought did but forerun my need,
And this same needy man must sell it me.
As I remember, this should be the house.   55
Being holiday, the beggar's shop is shut.
What ho! Apothecary!   *Enter Apothecary.*

Apothecary	Who calls so loud?
Romeo	Come hither man. I see that thou art poor,

Hold, there is forty ducats, let me have
A dram of poison, such soon-speeding gear   60
As will disperse itself through all the veins,
That the life-weary taker may fall dead
And that the trunk may be discharged of breath
As violently as hasty powder fired
Doth hurry from the fatal cannon's womb.   65

Apothecary	Such mortal drugs I have, but Mantua's law
	Is death to any he that utters them.
Romeo	Art thou so bare and full of wretchedness,

And fear'st to die? Famine is in thy cheeks,
Need and oppression starveth in thy eyes,   70
Contempt and beggary hangs upon thy back.
The world is not thy friend, nor the world's law.
The world affords no law to make thee rich.
Then be not poor, but break it, and take this.

Apothecary	My poverty, but not my will, consents. 75
Romeo	I pay thy poverty, and not thy will.
Apothecary	Put this in any liquid thing you will
	And drink it off, and if you had the strength

35 Let's see for means: how can I do it
35 mischief: evil
37 apothecary: someone who prepared and sold medicines
38 hereabouts 'a dwells: he lives around here
38 which late I noted: I saw him recently
39 tattered weeds: ragged clothes
39 overwhelming brows: overgrown, uncared for eyebrows
40 Culling of simples: picking herbs for medicines
40 Meagre were his looks: he looked thin
42 needy: run-down
45 A beggarly account of: a few tattered
46 bladders: used to hold liquids
47 packthread: string
47 cakes of roses: pressed rose petal bars
49 penury: obvious lack of money
51 present death: punishable by immediate execution
52 a caitiff wretch: a poor man desperate enough
53 forerun: run ahead of
56 holiday: a saint's day, no one worked

59 ducats: gold coins

60 dram: a small quantity
60 soon-speeding gear: stuff that works fast
63 the trunk: the body
63 discharged of breath: stop breathing
64 hasty powder: gunpowder
65 cannon's womb: inside of the cannon
66 mortal: deadly
67 he that utters: man that sells
68 bare: poor
69 And fear'st: yet still fear

71 Contempt and beggary hangs upon thy back: how the world despises you is clear from the pitiful state of your clothes
73 affords: gives you

75 My poverty, but not my will, consents: poverty forces me to take it, but I don't want to

	Of twenty men, it would dispatch you straight.		79 **dispatch you straight:** kill you instantly

Romeo There is thy gold, worse poison to men's souls, 80
Doing more murder in this loathsome world
Than these poor compounds that thou mayst not sell.
I sell thee poison, thou hast sold me none.
Farewell, buy food, and get thyself in flesh. —
— Come, cordial and not poison, go with me 85
To Juliet's grave, for there must I use thee. *They exit.*

82 **poor compounds:** wretched mixtures
84 **get thyself in flesh:** put some flesh on your bones
85 **cordial:** medicine to make you well

exam SKILLS

Target skill: interpreting character

You will strengthen your essay responses if you can cross-reference characters and events. Shakespeare's main characters usually develop during the course of the play's action. Cross-referencing a character at different points in the play demonstrates your confidence. It shows that you know the play well and understand the complexities of major characters.

Romeo's character does not stay constant throughout the play. He seems a romantic dreamer at the outset but becomes more headstrong by the end. Read Act 5 Scene 1. Here, Romeo is determined; railing against fate, issuing commands and making choices. Below are three quotes from Act 1 Scene 1 that present Romeo as a melancholy dreamer. Find three statements from Act 5 Scene 1 that present him as a very different character.
• "Adding to clouds more clouds with his deep sighs."
• "Shuts up his windows, locks fair daylight out."
• "sad hours seem long."

Director's Note, 5.1

✔ In Mantua, Romeo gets a message from a servant, telling him that Juliet is dead.
✔ Romeo decides to go to Juliet's tomb, and kill himself there, to be with her.
✔ He buys poison from an Apothecary.
✔ The audience know to expect a message to Romeo from Friar Lawrence. How might that affect the audience as this scene develops?

ACT 5 SCENE 2

Enter Friar John and Friar Lawrence by different doors.

Friar John Holy Franciscan friar, brother, ho!

Friar Lawrence This same should be the voice of Friar John.
Welcome from Mantua, what says Romeo?
Or, if his mind be writ, give me his letter.

Friar John Going to find a barefoot brother out, 5
One of our order, to associate me,
Here in this city visiting the sick,
And finding him, the searchers of the town
Suspecting that we both were in a house
Where the infectious pestilence did reign, 10
Sealed up the doors, and would not let us forth,
So that my speed to Mantua there was stayed.

Friar Lawrence Who bare my letter then to Romeo?

Friar John I could not send it — here it is again —
Nor get a messenger to bring it thee, 15
So fearful were they of infection.

4 **if his mind be writ:** if he's written to me
5 **barefoot brother:** Franciscan friar
6 **associate me:** travel with me (friars were supposed to travel in pairs)
8 **searchers:** official who viewed dead bodies to find the cause of death
10 **pestilence:** plague
11 **forth:** out
12 **my speed to Mantua there was stayed:** I couldn't go to Mantua
13 **bare:** took
15 **Nor get:** nor could I get

Friar Lawrence	Unhappy fortune! By my brotherhood,	
	The letter was not nice but full of charge,	
	Of dear import, and the neglecting it	
	May do much danger. Friar John, go hence,	20
	Get me an iron crow and bring it straight	
	Unto my cell.	
Friar John	Brother, I'll go and bring it thee.	*He exits.*
Friar Lawrence	Now must I to the monument alone,	
	Within this three hours will fair Juliet wake,	
	She will beshrew me much that Romeo	25
	Hath had no notice of these accidents.	
	But I will write again to Mantua,	
	And keep her at my cell till Romeo come.	
	Poor living corse, closed in a dead man's tomb!	30

Enter Paris and his Page, who carries flowers and a torch.

Paris	Give me thy torch, boy. Hence, and stand aloof,	
	Yet put it out, for I would not be seen.	
	Under yond yew trees lay thee all along,	
	Holding thy ear close to the hollow ground,	
	So shall no foot upon the churchyard tread,	5
	Being loose, unfirm with digging up of graves,	
	But thou shalt hear it. Whistle then to me,	
	As signal that thou hearest some thing approach.	
	Give me those flowers. Do as I bid thee, go.	
Page	[*Aside.*] I am almost afraid to stand alone	10
	Here in the churchyard, yet I will adventure.	

The Page moves away. Paris strews the grave with flowers.

Paris	Sweet flower, with flowers thy bridal bed I strew.	
	O woe, thy canopy is dust and stones,	
	Which with sweet water nightly I will dew,	
	Or wanting that, with tears distilled by moans.	15
	The obsequies that I for thee will keep,	
	Nightly shall be to strew thy grave and weep.	

The Page whistles.

	The boy gives warning, something doth approach,	
	What cursèd foot wanders this way tonight,	
	To cross my obsequies and true love's rite?	20
	What, with a torch? Muffle me, night, awhile.	

Paris moves away. Enter Romeo and Balthasar, with a torch, mattock, and an iron crow-bar.

Romeo	Give me that mattock and the wrenching iron.	
	Hold, take this letter. Early in the morning	
	See thou deliver it to my lord and father.	
	Give me the light. Upon thy life, I charge thee,	25
	Whate'er thou hear'st or seest, stand all aloof,	
	And do not interrupt me in my course.	
	Why I descend into this bed of death	
	Is partly to behold my lady's face,	
	But chiefly to take thence from her dead finger	30

18 nice: trivial
18 charge: serious information
19 Of dear import: vitally important
21 an iron crow: a crow-bar
21 straight: at once
24 the monument: the Capulet tomb
26 beshrew me much: abuse me
27 these accidents: what's happened
30 corse: corpse

Director's Note, 5.2

✔ Friar John tells Friar Lawrence he was not able to deliver the message to Romeo.
✔ Friar Lawrence rushes to Juliet's tomb, so she does not wake alone.

1 stand aloof: wait over there
2 Yet put it out: put the torch out
3 Under yond yew trees ... along: lie on the ground under those yew trees
6 Being: because it is

10 stand: stay
11 adventure: risk it

12 Sweet flower: Juliet
12 strew: scatter
13 canopy: bed covering
14 sweet water: perfumed water
14 dew: sprinkle
15 wanting: lacking
15 distilled: made from
16 obsequies: memorial rites

20 cross: interrupt
21 Muffle me: hide me

22 mattock: digging tool
22 wrenching iron: crow-bar
23 Hold: wait
25 charge: command
26 all aloof: well away
27 my course: what I'm doing

exam SKILLS

Target skill: understanding themes

Question: How does this scene help the audience to understand the theme of death in the play?

Action: Death is a significant theme here. Juliet's faked death draws Paris and Romeo to the vault, Paris thinks that Tybalt's murder caused Juliet to die, and Paris is killed by Romeo, who then kills himself.

Structure: The order of the deaths also heightens the tension. The audience will not be as affected by Paris' death as they will by Romeo's. When Paris confronts Romeo at the mouth of Juliet's tomb, it shows Romeo being emotionally generous to a rival as he pleads with Paris to leave. This makes us regret these deaths even more.

Setting: The setting is clearly fitting, taking place among the graves of the churchyard, at the entrance to the Capulet family vault. It is night time, adding to the sense of fear.

Language: The language of the scene is linked to death.

- What is the effect of the vault's opening being described as a mouth and stomach in lines 45–48?
- In his speech (lines 74–87) Romeo asks himself a series of questions. What is the impact of these?
- How does Romeo's comment that Paris is "One writ with me in sour misfortune's book" link with earlier references to fate and fortune?

Using the insights you have gained, answer the question above, considering the scene up to line 120.

	A precious ring, a ring that I must use	
	In dear employment. Therefore hence, be gone.	
	But if thou, jealous, dost return to pry	
	In what I further shall intend to do,	
	By heaven I will tear thee joint by joint,	35
	And strew this hungry churchyard with thy limbs.	
	The time and my intents are savage-wild,	
	More fierce and more inexorable far	
	Than empty tigers, or the roaring sea.	
Balthasar	I will be gone, sir, and not trouble you.	40
Romeo	So shalt thou show me friendship. Take thou that,	
	[He gives Balthasar money.]	
	Live and be prosperous, and farewell, good fellow.	
Balthasar	*[Aside.]* For all this same, I'll hide me hereabout,	
	His looks I fear, and his intents I doubt. *[Moves away.]*	
	Romeo starts to open the tomb.	
Romeo	Thou detestable maw, thou womb of death,	45
	Gorged with the dearest morsel of the earth.	
	Thus I enforce thy rotten jaws to open,	
	And in despite I'll cram thee with more food.	
Paris	This is that banished haughty Montague,	
	That murdered my love's cousin, with which grief	50
	It is supposèd, the fair creature died,	
	And here is come to do some villainous shame	
	To the dead bodies. I will apprehend him.	
	[Steps out.]	
	Stop thy unhallowed toil, vile Montague,	
	Can vengeance be pursued further than death?	55
	Condemnèd villain, I do apprehend thee.	
	Obey and go with me, for thou must die.	

31-2 I must use In dear employment: I need for an important purpose

33 jealous: suspicious

38 inexorable: unstoppable

39 empty tigers: hungry tigers

44 His looks I fear, and his intents I doubt: I don't like the look of him, I fear he might do something desperate

45 maw: stomach

46 Gorged with the dearest morsel of the earth: full, having taken the most precious thing on earth (Juliet)

48 in despite: despite the fact you're full

48 more food: another dead body (himself)

51 the fair creature: Juliet

53 apprehend: arrest

54 unhallowed toil: unholy work (breaking into the tomb)

Romeo	I must indeed, and therefore came I hither.	
	Good gentle youth, tempt not a desperate man.	
	Fly hence and leave me. Think upon these gone,	60
	Let them affright thee. I beseech thee, youth,	
	Put not another sin upon my head	
	By urging me to fury. O be gone!	
	By heaven, I love thee better than myself,	
	For I come hither armed against myself.	65
	Stay not, be gone, live, and hereafter say,	
	A madman's mercy bid thee run away.	
Paris	I do defy thy conjurations,	
	And apprehend thee for a felon here.	
Romeo	Wilt thou provoke me? Then have at thee, boy!	70

They fight.

Page	*[Aside.]* O Lord they fight! I will go call the watch. *[Exit.]*	
Paris	O I am slain! If thou be merciful,	
	Open the tomb, lay me with Juliet. *[He dies.]*	
Romeo	In faith I will, Let me peruse this face.	
	Mercutio's kinsman, noble County Paris!	75
	What said my man, when my betossèd soul	
	Did not attend him as we rode? I think	
	He told me Paris should have married Juliet.	
	Said he not so? Or did I dream it so?	
	Or am I mad, hearing him talk of Juliet,	80
	To think it was so? O give me thy hand,	
	One writ with me in sour misfortune's book.	
	I'll bury thee in a triumphant grave. *[Opens the grave.]*	
	A grave? O no, a lantern, slaughtered youth.	
	For here lies Juliet, and her beauty makes	85
	This vault a feasting presence full of light.	
	Death, lie thou there, by a dead man interred.	
	[Laying Paris in the tomb.]	
	How oft when men are at the point of death	
	Have they been merry? Which their keepers call	
	A light'ning before death? O how may I	90
	Call this a light'ning? O my love, my wife,	
	Death that hath sucked the honey of thy breath,	
	Hath had no power yet upon thy beauty.	
	Thou art not conquered. Beauty's ensign yet	
	Is crimson in thy lips and in thy cheeks,	95
	And Death's pale flag is not advancèd there.	
	Tybalt, liest thou there in thy bloody sheet?	
	O what more favour can I do to thee	
	Than with that hand that cut thy youth in twain	
	To sunder his that was thine enemy?	100
	Forgive me, cousin. Ah, dear Juliet,	
	Why art thou yet so fair? Shall I believe	
	That unsubstantial death is amorous,	
	And that the lean abhorrèd monster keeps	
	Thee here in dark to be his paramour?	105
	For fear of that, I still will stay with thee,	
	And never from this palace of dim night	

58 **therefore came I hither:** that's why I came here

59 **tempt not:** don't provoke

60 **these gone:** the dead in the tomb

65 **armed against myself:** to kill myself

68 **I do defy thy conjurations:** I won't listen to your appeals

69 **felon:** criminal

74 **peruse:** look at

76 **betossèd:** disturbed, whirling

77 **attend him:** listen to him

78 **should have:** was going to

82 **One writ with me in sour misfortune's book:** we've both been brought tragedy by fate

84 **a lantern:** a small tower on top of a building with glass on all sides to let in a lot of light

86 **feasting presence:** room where guests are welcomed before a feast

88 **at the point of death:** waiting for execution

89 **keepers:** jailers

90 **light'ning:** easing of sorrow

94 **ensign:** flag

96 **is not advancèd:** has not taken over

99 **cut thy youth in twain:** killed you while you were so young

100 **sunder his that was thine enemy:** end your enemy's (Romeo's) life

101 **cousin:** Tybalt

103–5 **unsubstantial death is amorous … his paramour:** skeleton-like Death loves you and keeps you here to be his lover

106 **still:** always

109

FROM THE REHEARSAL ROOM...

MONOLOGUE AS DUOLOGUE

In pairs, read Romeo's monologue as a duologue (lines 84–120), changing speaker at each punctuation mark.

1 What do you notice about Romeo's soliloquy?

2 Why does Romeo ask so many questions?

3 What effect do Romeo's questions have on the audience?

- Read the extract again. This time look for the significant changes in Romeo's speech – the places where his thoughts change.

- Divide the monologue into clearly defined sections, each block representing a change in Romeo's thoughts, a realisation, a decision and/ or an action.

- Once you have broken the speech into significant sections, add a title to each chunk of text, to sum up each section.

4 Looking at each section, how does Romeo begin to make sense of the sequence of events that have happened since his banishment?

5 What does Romeo see when he looks closely at Juliet?

6 What type of language and imagery does Romeo use to describe Juliet in death?

7 What options does Romeo believe that he has at this point in the play?

8 How does Romeo see death at this stage in the play? How does it differ from earlier in the play? Why has his opinion of death changed?

Depart again. Here, here will I remain
With worms that are thy chamber-maids. O here
Will I set up my everlasting rest   110
And shake the yoke of inauspicious stars
From this world-wearied flesh. Eyes, look your last.
Arms, take your last embrace. And lips, O you
The doors of breath, seal with a righteous kiss
A dateless bargain to engrossing Death.   *[Kisses her.]* 115
Come bitter conduct, come unsavoury guide,
Thou desperate pilot, now at once run on
The dashing rocks thy sea-sick weary bark.
Here's to my love!   *[He drinks.]*   O true apothecary,
Thy drugs are quick. Thus with a kiss I die.   *[He dies.]* 120

Enter Friar Lawrence, with a lantern, crowbar, and spade.

Friar Lawrence   Saint Francis be my speed! How oft tonight
Have my old feet stumbled at graves? Who's there?

Balthasar   Here's one, a friend, and one that knows you well.

Friar Lawrence   Bliss be upon you. Tell me, good my friend,
What torch is yond that vainly lends his light   125
To grubs and eyeless skulls? As I discern,
It burneth in the Capel's monument.

Balthasar   It doth so, holy sir, and there's my master,
One that you love.

Friar Lawrence   Who is it?

Balthasar   Romeo.

Friar Lawrence   How long hath he been there?

Balthasar   Full half an hour.   130

Friar Lawrence   Go with me to the vault.

Balthasar   I dare not, sir.
My master knows not but I am gone hence,
And fearfully did menace me with death
If I did stay to look on his intents.

Friar Lawrence   Stay then, I'll go alone. Fear comes upon me.   135
O much I fear some ill unthrifty thing.

Balthasar   As I did sleep under this yew tree here,
I dreamt my master and another fought,
And that my master slew him.

Friar Lawrence   Romeo!
He goes to the tomb, and sees blood and weapons on the ground.
Alack, alack, what blood is this, which stains   140
The stony entrance of this sepulchre?
What mean these masterless and gory swords
To lie discoloured by this place of peace?
                    [He enters the tomb.]
Romeo! O, pale! Who else? What, Paris too?
And steeped in blood? Ah, what an unkind hour   145
Is guilty of this lamentable chance?   *Juliet wakes.*
The lady stirs.

---

111 shake the yoke of inauspicious stars: throw off my unlucky fate

115 A dateless bargain to engrossing Death: an everlasting contract with Death who gets everything
116 conduct: guide
117 pilot: navigator that guides a ship into harbour
118 sea-sick weary bark: ship, sick of sailing (Romeo's body)
119 true: honest, truthful
121 be my speed: help me

124 Bliss be upon you: bless you
125 is yond: is that over there
126 As I discern: it seems to me

132 knows not but I am gone from hence: thinks I've gone away
133 fearfully did menace: threatened me in a very frightening way

136 some ill unthrifty thing: something dreadfully wasteful and evil

141 sepulchre: tomb
142 masterless: abandoned
142 gory: bloodstained
143 by this place of peace: near this tomb, where bodies lie at peace

145 unkind: cruel circumstance
146 this lamentable chance: tragic accidental meeting

Juliet and Romeo, 2004.

The stage direction for this kiss is in square brackets [ ]. This shows it is not in the printed text from Shakespeare's time. We have added it to help readers, by telling them what people in the theatre would see on stage.

1 Why did we put it at this exact point? Quote from the text to support your answer.

2 Are there any other places in this speech (lines 161–167) where a director could choose to have Juliet kiss Romeo? Again, quote to support your answer.

Kananu Kirimi, Tom Burke

Actor's view

Ellie Kendrick
Juliet, summer 2009

At first I played Juliet as being very confused and dazed, and then gradually, this horrible realisation dawns upon her, when she sees that everything is not quite right.

The Friar very hurriedly tells her that something terrible has happened, but then just runs away. And she gradually discovers the poison in his hand, and I think it is, obviously, a really heartbreaking moment. The lines speak for themselves here. I think the lines are much more affecting if they are spoken with real honesty. They are really heartbreaking. So we played it with Juliet almost subdued in grief here, and then she very quickly makes the decision to die herself.

I don't think Juliet would ever consider the Friar's suggestion of being hidden with the nuns. Romeo is the meaning of her life. She threatens to commit suicide earlier, and is deadly serious in that, and here she doesn't consider it for a moment, she says, 'Go, get thee hence, for I will not away.' In our production Juliet was very definite about that. Obviously very sad, but there is no doubt in her mind, that if Romeo is there, she needs to be there as well.

---

exam PREPARATION

Text focus: Act 5 Scene 3 lines 144–167

The exam essay question may be a thematic one, such as "How does Shakespeare present the theme of death in *Romeo and Juliet?*" This final scene of the play must be considered, as the action builds here to its dramatic conclusion.

The theme of death runs throughout the play. The audience was even told in the Prologue that the deaths of both Romeo and Juliet would occur and serve to "bury their parents' strife." The Exam Skills box on page 108 encouraged you to analyse the theme of death at the beginning of the scene.

Death links with other themes in the play. Some audience members might feel that the lovers' death comes because fate is not on their side: Tybalt kills Mercutio; Juliet's marriage is brought forward; the letter from Friar Lawrence is not delivered and the drug Juliet has taken wears off just too late to save Romeo. Others might feel that love is to blame, or that the family feud was bound to end in blood sacrifice.

(AO1) Response to characters and events:

- When Juliet finds the poison cup is empty, she tries to die by kissing the residue from Romeo's lips, and finally resorts to stabbing herself with his dagger. *Death was predicted in the Prologue, but the means was not. How do Juliet's attempts to kill herself add to the drama of the scene?*

- Despite having to search for a means of death, Juliet wakes and dies in the space of just 20 lines. *What is the effect of this event taking place so quickly?*

- The Friar's mixture of exclamation and questioning conveys the sense that things have gone horribly wrong. *Is he right to blame "a greater power than we" and "lamentable chance" rather than himself?*

(AO2) Language, structure and form:

- Juliet's language is filled with dramatic irony when she says, "I do remember well where I should be, and there I am. Where is my Romeo?" *How might the audience react to her words?*

- *Find examples of the following techniques in Juliet's speech in lines 161–170:*
  - *short sentences*
  - *the interrogative mood*
  - *the exclamatory mood*
  - *and comment on their effect.*

Question:

How does Shakespeare present Juliet's death?

Juliet	O comfortable Friar, where is my lord?
	I do remember well where I should be,
	And there I am. Where is my Romeo? 150

Friar Lawrence	I hear some noise lady. Come from that nest
	Of death, contagion, and unnatural sleep.
	A greater power than we can contradict
	Hath thwarted our intents. Come, come away.
	Thy husband in thy bosom there lies dead, 155
	And Paris too. Come, I'll dispose of thee
	Among a sisterhood of holy nuns.
	Stay not to question, for the watch is coming.
	Come, go, good Juliet, I dare no longer stay.

152 **contagion:** infectious disease

154 **thwarted our intents:** ruined our plans

156-7 **dispose of thee Among ... of holy nuns:** hide you in a nunnery

158 **Stay not to question:** don't ask questions now

Juliet	Go, get thee hence, for I will not away. 160
	Exit Friar Lawrence.
	What's here? A cup closed in my true love's hand?
	Poison, I see, hath been his timeless end.
	O churl, drunk all? And left no friendly drop
	To help me after? I will kiss thy lips,
	Haply some poison yet doth hang on them, 165
	To make me die with a restorative. *[Kisses him.]*
	Thy lips are warm.

162 **hath been his timeless end:** has killed him
163 **churl:** bad-mannered person
164 **To help me after:** for me to take to follow you (into death)
165 **Haply:** perhaps
166 **restorative:** double meaning: brings back to life; takes her to be with him

Enter Page and the Watch.

First Watchman	Lead boy, which way?
Juliet	Yea, noise? Then I'll be brief. O happy dagger!
	[Taking Romeo's dagger.]
	This is thy sheath, there rust, and let me die. 170

169 **brief:** quick
169 **happy:** found at just the right moment
170 **This:** her body

She stabs herself and falls.

Page	This is the place, there where the torch doth burn.
First Watchman	The ground is bloody, search about the churchyard.
	Go, some of you, whoe'er you find attach. *[Some exit.]*
	Pitiful sight! Here lies the County slain,
	And Juliet bleeding, warm, and newly dead 175
	Who here hath lain these two days burièd.
	Go tell the Prince, run to the Capulets,
	Raise up the Montagues. Some others search. *[More exit.]*
	We see the ground whereon these woes do lie,
	But the true ground of all these piteous woes 180
	We cannot without circumstance descry.

173 **whoe'er you find attach:** arrest anyone you find

179 **these woes:** Paris, Romeo and Juliet
180 **the true ground:** the reasons for
181 **without circumstance descry:** understand without more information

Enter some of the Watch, with Balthasar.

Second Watchman	Here's Romeo's man. We found him in the churchyard.
First Watchman	Hold him in safety, till the Prince come hither.

183 **in safety:** so he can't get away

Enter another Watchman and Friar Lawrence.

Third Watchman	Here is a friar, that trembles, sighs, and weeps.
	We took this mattock and this spade from him,
	As he was coming from this churchyard side. 185
First Watchman	A great suspicion, stay the friar too.

187 **A great suspicion, stay the friar too:** that looks very suspicious, don't let him go away

Enter the Prince, with attendants.

113

First Watchman (left of left-hand pillar), Capulet and Lady Capulet (left of grave), Romeo and Juliet, the Prince, and other Watchmen in the background, spring 2009.

1 Which are the earliest and latest lines at which this photo could have been taken? Explain your answer.

2 What are the two Watchmen at the back holding, and why?

3 Look back to page 3. Where was the photographer when he took this shot?

l–r Ben Aldridge, Vincent Brimble, Golda Rosheuvel, James Alexandrou, Lorraine Burroughs, Nick Khan

Prince	What misadventure is so early up, That calls our person from our morning's rest?

Enter Capulet and Lady Capulet.

Capulet	What should it be, that they so shriek abroad?
Lady Capulet	O the people in the street cry "Romeo", Some "Juliet", and some "Paris", and all run With open outcry toward our monument.
Prince	What fear is this which startles in your ears?
First Watchman	Sovereign, here lies the County Paris slain, And Romeo dead, and Juliet, dead before, Warm and new killed.
Prince	Search, seek, and know how this foul murder comes.
First Watchman	Here is a friar, and slaughtered Romeo's man, With instruments upon them, fit to open These dead men's tombs.
Capulet	O heavens! O wife, look how our daughter bleeds! This dagger hath mista'en, for, lo, his house Is empty on the back of Montague, And it mis-sheathed in my daughter's bosom!
Lady Capulet	O me, this sight of death, is as a bell That warns my old age to a sepulchre. *Enter Montague.*
Prince	Come Montague, for thou art early up To see thy son and heir now early down.
Montague	Alas, my liege, my wife is dead tonight, Grief of my son's exile hath stopped her breath. What further woe conspires against mine age?
Prince	Look, and thou shalt see.
Montague	O thou untaught! What manners is in this, To press before thy father to a grave?
Prince	Seal up the mouth of outrage for a while, Till we can clear these ambiguities, And know their spring, their head, their true descent. And then will I be general of your woes, And lead you even to death. Meantime forbear, And let mischance be slave to patience. Bring forth the parties of suspicion.
Friar Lawrence	I am the greatest, able to do least, Yet most suspected, as the time and place Doth make against me, of this direful murder. And here I stand, both to impeach and purge, Myself condemnèd, and myself excused.
Prince	Then say at once what thou dost know in this.
Friar Lawrence	I will be brief, for my short date of breath Is not so long as is a tedious tale. Romeo, there dead, was husband to that Juliet, And she, there dead, that's Romeo's faithful wife.

188 **What misadventure is so early up:** what awful thing has happened this early

190 **What should it be, that they so shriek abroad?:** what is everyone yelling about?

194 **What fear is this which startles in your ears?:** what are you frightened of?

200 **instruments:** tools

203 **hath mista'en:** has lost its way
203 **his house:** the dagger's sheath
204 **Montague:** Romeo
205 **it:** the dagger

207 **warns my old age to a sepulchre:** calls me to my grave

209 **early down:** dead before you were up
210 **is dead tonight:** died in the night
211 **Grief of:** grief over
214 **thou untaught:** rude boy
215 **To press before:** to push in front of
216 **Seal up the mouth of outrage:** quieten your grief
217 **clear these ambiguities:** find out what happened
218 **their spring, their head, their true descent:** what caused these events
219 **be general of your woes:** lead you in mourning and punish those responsible
220 **even to death:** executing the guilty if necessary
220 **forbear:** keep your feelings under control
221 **let mischance be slave to patience:** let patience rule your misery
222 **parties of suspicion:** suspects
223 **the greatest:** the most suspected
225 **Doth make against me:** throw suspicion on me
226 **impeach:** accuse
226 **purge:** clear (of blame)
229 **my short date of breath:** the short time I have left to live

190 195 200 205 210 215 220 225 230

115

FROM THE REHEARSAL ROOM...

SOME SHALL BE...PUNISHÈD

A number of characters could be blamed for the deaths of Romeo and Juliet. Working in groups of four, pick a character, one acts as prosecutor, one defends, and the other two are the jury.

- **Capulet** is guilty because of his foolish feuding and because he was such a heartless father.
- **Tybalt** is guilty because he set out to pick a quarrel and his cowardly killing of Mercutio forced Romeo to retaliate.
- **Montague** is guilty because he encouraged the family feuding, set a bad example and did not keep an eye on his son.
- **Lady Capulet** is guilty because she never took her daughter's side and cared more for society's feelings than for Juliet's.
- **Paris** is guilty because he was ready to force himself upon Juliet although he knew she did not love him. His desire to marry sparked the crisis.
- **Mercutio** is guilty because he was too eager to pick a fight and his death precipitated the tragedy by forcing Romeo to kill Tybalt.
- **The Prince** is guilty because his poor rule in Verona meant banishment for Romeo and this caused the death of the lovers.
- **The Nurse** is guilty because without her as their go-between, Juliet and Romeo could not have married.

1 Try your character. Research your case, (include at least three quotations). Try it, what is the verdict? If you have time, swap over so the jury now prosecute and defend, pick another character, and have another trial.

2 Discuss whether Romeo and Juliet themselves must bear some or much of the blame.

3 Had Shakespeare been available as judge, what do you think his verdict might have been?

I married them, and their stol'n marriage-day	233 **stol'n:** secret
Was Tybalt's doomsday, whose untimely death	234 **Tybalt's doomsday:** the day Tybalt died
Banished the new-made bridegroom from this city, 235	
For whom (and not for Tybalt) Juliet pined.	
You, to remove that siege of grief from her,	237 **that siege of grief from her:** the grief that shut her up
Betrothed, and would have married her perforce	238 **perforce:** by force
To County Paris. Then comes she to me,	
And with wild looks bid me devise some means 240	240 **devise some means:** work out a way
To rid her from this second marriage,	
Or in my cell there would she kill herself.	
Then gave I her (so tutored by my art)	243 **so tutored by my art:** as I have learned from my studies
A sleeping potion, which so took effect	
As I intended, for it wrought on her 245	245–6 **wrought on her The form of death:** made her seem dead
The form of death. Meantime, I writ to Romeo,	
That he should hither come as this dire night,	247 **as:** on
To help to take her from her borrowed grave,	
Being the time the potion's force should cease.	
But he which bore my letter, Friar John, 250	
Was stayed by accident, and yesternight	
Returned my letter back. Then all alone,	
At the prefixèd hour of her waking,	253 **prefixèd:** prearranged
Came I to take her from her kindred's vault,	
Meaning to keep her closely at my cell 255	255 **closely:** hidden
Till I conveniently could send to Romeo.	
But when I came some minute ere the time	257 **ere:** before
Of her awaking, here untimely lay	
The noble Paris and true Romeo dead.	259 **true:** faithful
She wakes, and I entreated her come forth,	260 **entreated:** begged
And bear this work of heaven with patience 260	261 **this work of heaven:** what has happened

But then a noise did scare me from the tomb,
And she, too desperate, would not go with me,
But, as it seems, did violence on herself.
All this I know, and to the marriage   265
Her nurse is privy. And if aught in this
Miscarried by my fault, let my old life
Be sacrificed, some hour before his time,
Unto the rigour of severest law.

Prince   We still have known thee for a holy man.   270
Where's Romeo's man? What can he say to this?

Balthasar   I brought my master news of Juliet's death,
And then in post he came from Mantua
To this same place, to this same monument.
This letter he early bid me give his father,   275
And threatened me with death, going in the vault,
If I departed not, and left him there.

Prince   Give me the letter, I will look on it.
Where is the County's Page, that raised the watch?
Sirrah, what made your master in this place?   280

Page   He came with flowers to strew his lady's grave,
And bid me stand aloof, and so I did.
Anon comes one with light to ope the tomb,
And by and by my master drew on him,
And then I ran away to call the watch.   285

Prince   This letter doth make good the Friar's words,
Their course of love, the tidings of her death.
And here he writes that he did buy a poison
Of a poor 'pothecary, and therewithal
Came to this vault to die, and lie with Juliet.   290
Where be these enemies? Capulet, Montague?
See what a scourge is laid upon your hate
That heaven finds means to kill your joys with love.
And I, for winking at your discords too,
Have lost a brace of kinsmen. All are punished.   295

Capulet   O brother Montague, give me thy hand,
This is my daughter's jointure, for no more
Can I demand.

Montague   But I can give thee more.
For I will raise her statue in pure gold,
That while Verona by that name is known,   300
There shall no figure at such rate be set
As that of true and faithful Juliet.

Capulet   As rich shall Romeo's by his lady's lie,
Poor sacrifices of our enmity.

Prince   A glooming peace this morning with it brings,   305
The sun, for sorrow, will not show his head.
Go hence, to have more talk of these sad things,
Some shall be pardoned, and some punishèd.
For never was a story of more woe
Than this of Juliet, and her Romeo.   *They all exit.* 310

266 **to the marriage her nurse is privy:** her nurse knew about the marriage
266 **aught in this miscarried:** anything went wrong
267 **some hour before his time:** before my natural time to die
268 **Unto the rigour of severest law:** as the harshest possible punishment
270 **still have known thee:** have always thought you were
272 **in post:** as fast as possible
274 **early:** early the next morning
275 **going in:** as he went into
279 **made your master:** was your master doing
282 **Anon comes one:** just then someone arrived
283 **by and by:** soon after
285 **make good:** confirm
288 **therewithal:** with it (the poison)
291 **scourge:** punishment
292 **your joys:** your children
293 **winking at your discords:** letting you quarrel so
294 **a brace:** a pair, two
291 **jointure:** payment made to the bridegroom's family by the bride's family on marriage
300 **There shall no figure at such rate be set:** no one will be seen as more important
301 **Romeo's:** a statue to Romeo
302 **Poor sacrifices to our enmity:** both victims of our hatred
304 **glooming:** dark, clouded

Director's Note, 5.3

✔ Paris and Romeo fight outside Juliet's tomb. Romeo kills Paris.
✔ Romeo enters the tomb, and drinks poison, kissing Juliet as he dies.
✔ Friar Lawrence arrives; Juliet wakes and sees Romeo's body.
✔ They hear a noise. The Friar flees. Juliet stabs herself.
✔ The Watchmen arrive followed by the Prince, the Capulets and Montague.
✔ Friar Lawrence tells what happened. Montague and Capulet end the feud.
✔ The Prince says, 'Some shall be pardoned, and some punished.' Who should be punished?

Act and Scene plot summary

1	The Prologue introduces the play with its themes of fate, love, and death.
1.1	Montagues and Capulets fight in the street. The Prince orders them to stop and threatens that any further fighting will be punishable by death. Romeo admits to Benvolio that he is in love with Rosaline.
1.2	Capulet tells Paris to woo Juliet, but that she is too young to marry. Benvolio persuades Romeo to go the Capulet's feast, in disguise, where he will find Rosaline and other women who are as beautiful.
1.3	Lady Capulet tells Juliet and the Nurse that Paris wants to marry Juliet.
1.4	Mercutio mocks Romeo for being in love. Benvolio urges them to go to the Capulet ball.
1.5	Romeo and his friends arrive disguised at the Capulet ball. Tybalt recognises and would attack the enemy Romeo, but is stopped by Capulet. Tybalt plans revenge. Romeo and Juliet meet and fall in love. They then learn that they are the children of the feuding families.
2	The Chorus confirms that Romeo and Juliet are in love and are determined to be together at any cost.
2.1	Benvolio and Mercutio look for Romeo who has hidden from them.
2.2	Romeo overhears Juliet speak of her love for him. He tells her that he loves her. They agree to marry.
2.3	Romeo tells Friar Lawrence that he is no longer in love with Rosaline but is in love with Juliet. Lawrence eventually agrees to marry them.
2.4	Mercutio, Benvolio and Romeo meet. Romeo gives the Nurse a message for Juliet with the news that Lawrence will marry them that afternoon at his cell.
2.5	The Nurse gives Juliet the message.
2.6	Juliet meets Romeo at Friar Lawrence's cell. They leave with Lawrence to be married.
3.1	Tybalt tries to provoke a fight with Romeo; Mercutio fights Tybalt instead and is fatally wounded. Romeo, ashamed, challenges Tybalt and kills him. Romeo flees. The Prince orders Romeo's banishment.
3.2	Juliet longs for Romeo. The Nurse tells her of Tybalt's death, and of Romeo's banishment. Juliet despairs but the Nurse tells her she will bring Romeo to her, secretly, that night.
3.3	Friar Lawrence tells Romeo that he has been banished. Distraught, Romeo attempts suicide. Friar Lawrence sends Romeo to Juliet but tells him he must leave for Mantua before daybreak.
3.4	Capulet tells Paris that he can marry Juliet in 3 days' time.
3.5	After spending the night with Juliet, Romeo leaves for Mantua. Lady Capulet tells Juliet she must marry Paris; Juliet refuses; Capulet threatens to disown her. The Nurse advises Juliet to marry Paris.
4.1	Juliet meets Paris at Friar Lawrence's cell. Paris leaves. Friar Lawrence comes up with a plan: she should agree to marry Paris but take a drug that will make everyone think she has died. Friar Lawrence will tell Romeo and they will wait for her in the tomb until she awakes and then take her away.
4.2	Juliet returns home and tells her parents that she will marry Paris. Capulet moves the wedding forward to Wednesday.
4.3	Juliet sends her mother and the Nurse away and goes to bed. She takes the drug.
4.4	Capulet, his wife, and the Nurse prepare for the wedding.
4.5	The Nurse finds Juliet, all believe she is dead. Friar Lawrence starts to arrange the funeral.
5.1	In Mantua Romeo receives a message that Juliet is dead and has been put in the family tomb. He buys poison intending to kill himself by her side.
5.2	Friar Lawrence discovers that Romeo has not received his message and hurries to Juliet's tomb.
5.3	Paris fights Romeo in Juliet's tomb. Paris is killed. Romeo takes the poison. Friar Lawrence arrives; Juliet wakes and finds Romeo dead. They hear a noise. Friar Lawrence flees and Juliet stabs herself. The Watch arrive and Friar Lawrence and Balthasar are arrested. The Prince, the Capulets and Montague arrive. Friar Lawrence reveals what has happened. The families agree to end their feud.

Key terms

These key terms provide a starting place for exploring key aspects of *Romeo and Juliet*. At GCSE, your teacher will tell you which examples are most relevant to how your Shakespeare response will be assessed.

THEMES AND IDEAS

Conflict

The long running feud between the Capulets and Montagues Prologue 1–5 Despite the Veronan law, both sides continue 1.1.35–45 The feud directly causes the deaths of Mercutio 3.1.87, Tybalt 3.1.129, Paris 5.3.54–73, and, indirectly, the deaths of Romeo: 5.3.120 and Juliet: 5.3.169–70 Some characters work for peace; e.g. the Prince 1.1.74–90, Benvolio 1.1.58–9, Lady Montague 1.1.72–3; others revel in the conflict; e.g. Sampson and Gregory 1.1.36–45, Tybalt 1.1.63–5 Characters experience internal conflict, e.g. over loyalties – Juliet when Romeo is Tybalt's murderer 3.2.73–9, Romeo over fighting Tybalt 3.1.59–69 until Mercutio is slain 3.1.120–30

Love

Courtly love

Romeo's idealistic, unrequited love for Rosaline 1.1.203–232 makes him avoid friends 1.1.116–124, moody 1.1.126–134 secretive 1.1.141–6, sad 1.1.183–9, powerless and unfulfilled 1.1.203–19 and suffer 1.3.55–8 It amuses Romeo's friends 2.1.8–22; 2.4.13–5 Romeo believes it blinds him to other womens' charms 1.1.227–231 and 1.2.88–93

Arranged marriages

Common in Shakespeare's time, Capulet's choice for Juliet, Paris, strengthens family ties and transfers wealth. Capulet believes arranged marriages should not be entered into too early 1.2.12–3 and tells acceptable suitor, Paris, to win Juliet's 'heart' 1.2.16–9 Lady Capulet asks Juliet if she can choose to love Paris who offers status and wealth 1.3.75–91 Juliet agrees to try to obey her parent's wishes 1.3.93–5 After Juliet falls in love with Romeo she is unable to choose to be in love with Paris instead. When Juliet refuses Paris, Capulet tries to force Juliet to obey by threatening to banish her 3.5.192–4

Passionate love

Natural, and more powerful than either hatred, death 2.2.66–84 or family ties 3.2.96–126 It overcomes boundaries of family feuds 2.2.51 and 2.2.69, reconciles individuals 2.2.144; 2.3.49–54 and, potentially, their families when Romeo turns from foe to friend 3.1.59–61 It makes lovers happy 2.4.49–79, strengthens characters 4.2.125, is worth risking death for 2.2.76–8, 82–4 and is fulfilled by marriage; but if it is too strong, it is dangerous 2.6.9–16: thwarted, it leads to the deaths of Romeo 5.3.120 and Juliet 5.3.169–70

Lust

Source of comedy in bawdy jokes 46–53; act of hate 1.1.14–6; a response of the eyes and so easily changes its focus 1.2.47–51; 1.2.96–9; contrasts with the fidelity and purity of Romeo and Juliet's passionate love 2.2.35–9

Hatred

Drives the feud 1.1.11–69, contrasts with love and peace 1.1.63–5, results in bloodshed, and must be constrained by the law 1.1.76–90; it drives Lady Capulet to seek Romeo's execution 3.1.175–180, Tybalt to duel with Romeo, and, later, Paris. It is punished with loss 5.3.293–5

Fate and fortune

The Prologue describes Romeo and Juliet as 'star–crossed lovers' coming from 'fatal loins' whose 'death–marked' future is frequently foreshadowed in characters' speeches 1.4.107–114; 3.5.200–3 and in images 2.2.184 The characters express a sense of fate; e.g. Romeo 1.4.107–14; 2.6.6–8, Juliet 2.1 134–5; 3.2.21–2; 3.5.54–7 Juliet calls on fate to help 3.5.60–4 Friar Lawrence's speech foreshadows events 2.3.19–22. Romeo dreams Juliet finds him dead 5.1.6–8

Light and dark

Romeo brings light; e.g. to the dark masquerade ball 1.4.35–39; light is an image of time and life passing 1.4.43–5 Juliet is symbolised as light 2.2.2–4 True love is revealed in the darkness 2.2 and night is the time for passion 3.2.1–31 Dawn heralds Romeo's departure 3.5.9–15 and misery 3.5.36 The final tragic suicides and deaths all take place in the darkness of the vault

Secrecy/concealment

Lovesick Romeo conceals himself from Benvolio 1.1.117–124, and 2.1 and the reason for his unhappiness 1.1.138 Romeo hides his identity to attend the Capulet's masked ball 1.5; he hides below Juliet's balcony 2.2 and overhears her declaration of love 2.2.33–49 There are secret meetings 2.4.160–3, a secret marriage 2.5 and secret plans 2.5.72 Juliet conceals her love for Romeo 3.5.81–3, marriage 3.5, 4.1.19, grief at Romeo's banishment 3.5.76–7, and plans to avoid marrying Paris 3.5.241–2 Father Lawrence's secret plan 4.2.89–120 will conceal the lovers. Drugged Juliet is concealed in the tomb to wait for Romeo

Time

The play's events are compressed into four days. Images of time passing include death 1.2.14–15, loss of light 1.4.43–5, birds; i.e. nightingale symbolises night, lark day 3.5.1–6 The time for stars is the time for love 1.2.25 Events are often foreshadowed 1.2.86–8 Characters set appointments 2.2.169 which are thwarted 2.5.1–3; yearning makes time seem long 2.2.170 Capulet forces Juliet to marry Paris quickly 3.5 188–94 leads to Father Lawrence's poison plot 4.1.68 and the lovers' deaths.

Events overlap creating irony; e.g. as Capulet fixes Thursday as the date of Juliet's marriage to Paris, upstairs Romeo and Juliet consummate their marriage 3.4 and 3.5 News of Juliet's 'death' reaches Romeo before the letter from Friar Lawrence 5.1.17–21

Gender

Men fight 1.1.55, feud 1.1.87–90, hold power as fathers 1.2.17–9 and political leaders 1.1.89–90, use women to cement relationships, transfer wealth and secure family bonds and status through arranged marriages 1.2.12–3 Romeo fears his love for Juliet makes him 'effeminate' 3.1.112–13 but he goes on to avenge Mercutio's death by slaying Tybalt. Women are objects of desire 1.5.42–51, meant to obey fathers 3.4.13, 159–62, 4.2.22 and husbands 4.2.41 Female rule, shown by Queen Mab, only causes dreams of wish fulfilment and madness 1.4.55–95

Religion and myths

Images of pagan classical Greek and Roman deities are associated with courtly love 2.1.11–15; e.g. Cupid, giving lovers 'wings' and skill at dancing 1.4.17–18, then causes unrequited lover's suffering 1.4.19–22; Dian the virgin huntress 1.1.204 Queen Mab is associated with dreams, wish fulfilment and madness 1.4.55–95 Courtly love is a religion 1.2.88–93, replaced by Romeo and Juliet's pure, passionate love which is associated with Christian imagery: pilgrims, saints, shrines 1.5.92–105, sin and purification 1.5.106

Appearance and reality

Rosaline appears the ideal woman 1.2.88–93, 2.1.18–20, until Romeo sees Juliet 1.5.42–51 Juliet only appears ready to obey and marry Paris 3.5.233–5; she will only appear dead 4.1.93–108 Romeo believes drugged Juliet really is dead 5.3.91–105 The Prince asks for reality to be explained by Benvolio 3.1.150–174 and Friar Lawrence 5.3.231–264

Youth versus age

Age is associated with withering 1.2.11, canker, the roots of the feud 1.1.88, no longer dancing 1.5.29 In Friar Lawrence age brings wisdom love, faith 2.3.1–44, 4.5.65–76 Youth is associated with fighting 1.1.55–65, 3.1.86, 5.3.71, strong emotions, true love 2.2.90–135, 2.4.49–79, passion 3.2.1–28, despair 3.3.29–47, courage 4.3.20–57 and death 1.1.55–65, 3.1.86, 5.3.71, 5.3.120, 5.3.169–70

Order versus chaos

Order, such as the implementing of law 1.1.89–90, 3.1.184–195, 3.1.184–196, arranged marriages, or traditions of courtly love maintain peace and stability. If order is disrupted it leads to disorder/chaos; e.g. giving illiterate Peter a reading task 1.2.39–41; leads to Romeo gatecrashing the ball; Juliet marrying outside her father's choice leads to the tragedy

Death

Men duel and kill each other: 1.1.55–65, 3.1.86, 5.3.71 Death is the punishment for murder 1.1.89–90 but avenging murder leads to Romeo's banishment 3.1.185–196 Romeo and Juliet's love is death-marked Prologue Romeo foretells his death 1.4.108–14 Juliet foreshadows her suicide 2.1.134–7 and Romeo his 3.3.43–6 Juliet fears Romeo's death 3.5.54–7 and her own 4.3.31–4 Both Romeo and Juliet threaten to kill themselves, Romeo: 3.3.107–9; 5.1.34–35; Juliet: 3.5.244 and 4.1.54, 4.1.76–85 and do so, Romeo: 5.3.120, Juliet: 5.3.169–70

CHARACTERISATION AND VOICE

Characterisation
The skill of making an actor playing a part do it so well that the audience believes he is a real person, with a distinct personality, attitude, feelings and behaviour. Characterisation can be reported such as Romeo's 1.1.125–136, or revealed; e.g . the Nurse's rambling prose.1.3.18–44

Voice see Examiner's Tips p 34

LANGUAGE

Alliteration
Words begin with same sounds: 'Now old desire doth in his death-bed lie' 2.1.1 'all my fortunes at thy foot I'll lay/And follow thee…' 2.2.147–81

Allusions
Indirect references to other texts especially the classics and mythology *see religion and myths*; e.g. the use of a Chorus echoes classical Greek dramas

Antithesis
The use of opposites such as light and dark; e.g. 'More light and light, more dark and dark our woes!' 3.5.36 Pairing of opposites in an expression is an oxymoron

Epithets
Sum up character's natures: The fiery Tybalt 1.1.102

Hyperbole
Exaggeration used to emphasize a point; e.g. Romeo's first descriptions of Juliet: 'The brightness of her cheek would shame those stars' 2.2.19

Iambic pentameter
A pattern of 5 pairs of unstressed then stressed syllables in a line; e.g. the Prologue and 'But soft! What light through yonder window breaks?'

Shared lines
Where different characters complete an iambic pentameter, increases the pace e.g. 2.2.25

Imagery
Language which creates impressions by association and suggestion. Romeo and Juliet's true love described using images

from the Christian religion; e.g. pilgrims, saints, shrines 1.5.92–105, 2.2.55, baptism, angels 2.2.26–32 Whereas courtly love is described through pagan and classical religion, ancient myths etc: 2.1.11–15; Juliet's beauty is associated with brilliant light 1.5.42 and 2.2.14–21. Unhappy love is associated with avoiding natural light 1.1.128–133 and darkness 1.1.133–5 Suffering love is associated with smoke, sea 3.5.130–7, an extended metaphor and madness 1.1.185–8, clouds 1.1.127, being weighed down unable to dance 1.4.14–6 Fiery images describe strong emotions; e.g. falling in love 1.5.42, rage 1.1.77 or characters driven by hate; e.g. fiery Tybalt 1.1.102 Animal imagery used as insults 1.1.7 and 10, feuding, hate driven men are beasts 1.1.76 Birds to compare women's beauty 1.2.87, 1.5.46, or time passing 3.5.1–6 Romeo wishes he were Juliet's bird 2.2.183 Poison 4.3.57, 5.3.119–20, 5.3.160–5

Irony
Because the Prologue and chorus reveal the plot, speeches foreshadowing future events can create irony; e.g. 'compare her [Rosaline's] face with some that I shall show, And I will make thee think thy swan a crow' 1.2.86–7 Swans are faithful, only having one mate, crows are birds of death. Romeo states he'll suffer if he stops loving Rosaline 1.2.88–93 Romeo's marriage will kill Juliet 2.1.134–5 Mercutio's death will lead to others 3.1.117–8 Juliet dreads waking too early 4.3.31–2 but wakes too late. After marrying Romeo, Juliet hides her true feelings creating dramatic irony 3.5. 96–102 Situational irony; e.g. events overlapping: while Capulet fixes Thursday for Juliet to marry Paris, upstairs, Romeo and Juliet consummate their marriage 3.4 and 3.5

Onomatopoeia
Where sounds of words echo their sense; e.g. 'Who, nothing hurt withal hiss'd him in scorn' 1.1.105

Oxymorons
Phrases made up of opposites such as 'Beautiful tyrant, fiend angelical', 'Ravenous dove-feathered raven! Wolvish–ravening lamb' 3.2.75–6

Personification
Words used to put human or animal characteristics onto non-human or animal things, e.g. 'limping winter treads' 1.2.28, death as Juliet's husband e.g. 'And death, not Romeo, take my maidenhead' 3.2.137

Rhyming couplets
Used to round off scenes Prologue, 1.3.100–1, 2.2. 189–90, create memorable exits 1.5.90–1, express heightened emotions; e.g. Romeo's speech at first seeing Juliet 1.5.42–3, Juliet's discovery she's in love with a Montague 1.5.1.137–40

Sonnets
14-line poems, in iambic pentameter

following a rhyme scheme – often ababcdcdefefgg. There are three in the play: The First Chorus (Prologue); Romeo and Juliet's first meeting, 1.5.92–105, the Second Chorus at the start of Act 2

Symbolism
Romeo carries the torch and so bears light, symbolic of bringing love and passion, into Juliet's house 1.4.12

Word play
E.g. 'sycamour' = sick amour 1.1.114 and 1.1.1–4 ; puns such as: **collier** (coal vendor) which sound like **choler** (anger) and **collar** (hangman's noose)

PERFORMANCE: STAGECRAFT AND THEATRICALITY

Stagecraft
Stage directions in text such as Benvolio commenting on putting on his mask 1.4.30–2 Clues in the text to guide actors; e.g. repetition of part suggests sword thrusts: 1.1.107; sound effects e.g. 'Hist' 2.2.159; the progression from Romeo kissing Juliet's hand, to their hands meeting and finally they kiss on the lips 1.5.92–106

Theatricality
Swordfights 1.1.and 3.1; dancing at masked ball 1.5.24; Romeo conceals himself below the balcony with Juliet appearing above 2.2

Soliloquy
Characters speaking alone to the audience reveal their inmost thoughts and feelings; e.g. 2.2.1–8, 3.2.1–31, 4.3.14–57

Suspense
Juxtaposition creates dramatic tension; e.g. at the ball, as Romeo speaks of falling in love with Juliet, his identity is discovered by his enemy, Tybalt 1.5.52

Symbolism
An idea is represented by an object; e.g. Romeo carries the torch and so bears light, symbolic of bringing love and passion, into Juliet's house 1.4.12

CONTEXTS

Contexts within the play that create a scene or mood.
Characters alone on stage seem more vulnerable and courageous; e.g. Juliet deciding to take the poison 4.3, and kill herself 5.3.161–70; grim atmosphere at the tomb where Tybalt, then Paris and finally Romeo and Juliet lie dead 5.3

Context around the play
For example, the way that ideas, customs and events of the period, are reflected in the play: *see notes on duelling, courtly love, arranged marriages.*

Context of performance
Where and how it is performed and how that affects the audience's understanding; e.g. characters in modern costume or Elizabethan dress